WHAT HAPPENS WHEN WE PRAY?

Does it make a difference?

JOHN SAXBEE

kevin
mayhew

kevin
mayhew

First published in Great Britain in 2016 by Kevin Mayhew Ltd
Buxhall, Stowmarket, Suffolk IP14 3BW
Tel: +44 (0) 1449 737978 Fax: +44 (0) 1449 737834
E-mail: info@kevinmayhew.com

www.kevinmayhew.com

9 8 7 6 5 4 3 2 1 0
ISBN 978 1 84867 826 2
Catalogue No. 1501512

Cover design by Rob Mortonson
© Images used under licence from Shutterstock Inc.
Edited by Nicki Copeland
Typeset by Melody-Anne Lee

Printed and bound in Great Britain

Contents

About the author

John Saxbee retired as Bishop of Lincoln in 2011. Born in Bristol, he studied at Bristol and Durham Universities. His doctoral research was on the writings of Søren Kierkegaard. He was ordained in 1972 and held parochial posts in Plymouth before being appointed Director of Training for the Diocese of Exeter and Joint Director of the South West Ministry Training Course. He was Bishop and Archdeacon of Ludlow for eight years before translation to Lincoln in 2001. His publications include *Liberal Evangelism* (SPCK, 1994) and *No Faith in Religion* (O Books, 2009). He reviews books on religion and philosophy for various journals. For Kevin Mayhew John has written *WayMARKers, A route map through Lent to Easter* (1501418) and has contributed to the following publications: *Faith Matters* (1501369), *Facing the Issues* (1501353) and *More Sermons on Difficult Subjects* (1501389).

Preface

What follows is a distillation of much that has been learned over many years from my own practice of prayer, and my reflection on some of the issues which have proved particularly challenging to my practice of petitionary and intercessory prayer. But, as always, the influence of others, both through personal engagement and via the printed page, has been vital in taking forward this quest for clarity and coherence.

While dealing with philosophical and theological ideas which can be complex and intellectually demanding, I hope I have made them as accessible as possible, but without over-simplification. Taking these kinds of issues a step at a time seems to work best, and I hope that questions raised as the argument develops will be answered in subsequent sections. As with prayer itself, there is merit in engaging at a considered pace with the issues it raises for theology, philosophy and day-to-day discipleship. Above all, it is a study with a pastoral purpose, touching as it does on matters which are as emotionally sensitive as they are intellectually intriguing. Most important of all is my hope and, yes, prayer that what follows will be not only an encouragement to think about what we are doing when we pray, but also a stimulus to pray with ever more conviction and commitment.

It will be noticed that I perpetuate the practice of using a male personal pronoun for God. This is a practice with which I feel increasingly uncomfortable, and I look forward to the time when an elegant alternative becomes available.

John Saxbee

Chapter one

Approaches to prayer

'I have been so often driven to my knees by the overwhelming conviction that I had nowhere else to go.'

So declared Abraham Lincoln, and we must be impressed by the humility of this great man who had the honesty to acknowledge his need to pray when his own resources were unequal to the challenges he faced. But his confession also confronts us with a challenge. For he seems to be treating prayer as the activity of last resort. All else has failed so he has no choice but to give prayer a chance.

To be fair to President Lincoln, he almost certainly did have a more sophisticated appreciation of what prayer is and means than this single quotation suggests. Yet the perception of prayer as a desperation measure to fall back on in times of greatest danger or perplexity is a familiar one. Most of us are likely to invoke God's aid, in however perfunctory a way, when our backs are to the wall and we are at our wits' end. But what are we doing when we utter those prayers? Indeed, what are we doing whenever we call upon God, whether in extremis or in the ordinary, everyday living of our lives?

To answer that question, we must first of all differentiate between the several kinds of prayer that are familiar to people of faith in general, and to Christians in particular. And we must do so conscious that we are touching on matters which we dare not treat lightly. We like the story of the little girl who fell to her knees in a sturdy box pew when the Vicar said, 'Let us pray,' and then nervously tugged on the sleeve of her mother's coat and asked who they were hiding from. She was right to be anxious. After all, the Bible confirms that 'It is a fearful thing to fall into the hands of the living God' (Hebrews 10:31).

Prayer is a serious business, and we must take it seriously. But some forms of prayer are more problematic than others, and identifying the more challenging of these will help us to put prayer in perspective and so clarify what it is you and I are doing when we pray.

For many years, a favourite gift for Confirmation candidates has been a little book entitled *In His Presence*. It was first published in 1901 and, notwithstanding updates from time to time, it consistently offers ACTS as the key to organising times of prayer: Adoration, Confession, Thanksgiving and Supplication are offered as pegs on which to hang an ordered life of prayer – and in that order.

So we begin by acknowledging the One to whom we pray. This can simply be seen as equivalent to addressing a letter by giving the recipient their proper title. Indeed, the opening of the Lord's Prayer has something of that feel about it: 'Our Father, who art in heaven'. However, there is usually more to it than that, and we go on to offer praise to God in words that do justice to God's grandeur: 'Hallowed be thy name.'

Next we acknowledge our unworthiness to approach One who is so worthy. We need to examine ourselves, give an account of our failings and invoke God's mercy and forgiveness – which is assured, but which we must never take for granted. Likewise, we should never take God's gifts and grace for granted, so we move into thanksgiving mode and express our gratitude for what the *Book of Common Prayer* describes as God's 'goodness and loving kindness'.

Up to this point we seem to be simply applying to our relationship with God the same courtesies we would normally extend to those people with whom we engage day by day. So we give praise where praise is due and look to grace our greeting with something affirming and complimentary. That is simply courteous, as are expressions of apology and contrition when we have wronged someone or distressed them in some way. It has been said that 'sorry' is the hardest word, but it is nevertheless necessary if we are to build and maintain healthy and durable relationships. Expressing gratitude is also a natural courtesy in our relationships with others. If 'sorry' is the hardest word to say, then 'thank you' are the easiest words to forget to say, and we think it a discourtesy when they are omitted.

So we can safely say that Adoration, Confession and Thanksgiving present few difficulties when it comes to what we are doing when we pray. Of course, questions have been asked about whether God feels the same way as we do about such courtesies, and why God would want people to do obeisance, mortify themselves for their sins and indulge in extravagant expressions of gratitude when, presumably, God has no need of such all too human reassurances. Yet whatever God may or may not want or need – and that is an issue to which we shall return – the fact remains that we feel and know these courtesies to be important ingredients for honest and mature relationships, and we would think it odd if they did not find their rightful place in our relationship with God.

That being the case, we will not dwell on these aspects of prayer in what follows. They are key components in an ordered approach to prayer, but the really tricky theological and philosophical issues relating to prayer arise in relation to that fourth element in our ACTS matrix – Supplication – and it is those issues which will feature most prominently in our analysis and explanations.

At this point, a disclaimer is in order. This is not a 'how to' book when it comes to prayer and praying. There are many excellent prayer manuals to guide us through different styles of prayer – Contemplative, Ignatian, Julian, *Lectio Divina*, etc. – and they also provide useful guidance when it comes to where, when and how to pray. Our focus will be upon the underlying provenance of prayer and the difficulties posed by a practice which provokes as many questions as it does answers, and which has been a stumbling block for sceptics and believers alike. The point was made with wit and admirable concision by Adam Leys in a letter to his favourite newspaper:

> I once tried to work out what would be the secular equivalent to a prayer and concluded that it was writing a letter to the *Guardian*. It contains a heartfelt wish, disappears up into the ether, and nothing happens.[1]

There is, of course, a lovely irony here insofar as Adam's letter does not disappear into the ether – it actually is published. Also, something does happen – not least, my quoting it in

---

1. *Guardian* letters, 24 June 2015.

this book! Still, he echoes widely held sentiments to the effect that prayer giving expression to 'a heartfelt wish' is ultimately futile and inconsequential because 'nothing happens'.

The poet R. S. Thomas writes about prayer in a poem significantly entitled *Folk Tale*. He likens prayer to gravel flung at a window to attract attention. However, the lack of any realistic chance of engagement between humanity and divinity seems to render the act of prayer futile. He himself would have given up a long time ago except that once, having flung his gravel-like prayers, he thought he saw the movement of a curtain . . .

This counters the assumption that nothing happens in response to our prayers, but it falls far short of a wholehearted endorsement of prayer as instrumental, and capable of changing the way things go in the world. There is the indiscriminate flinging of gravel with little expectation of a response, and no way of engaging with one even if it were to occur. Hope is vested in a momentary 'movement of a curtain', and this keeps the poet from giving up altogether.

So somewhere between our *Guardian* correspondent's extreme pessimism, R. S. Thomas' severely guarded optimism and a full-blown endorsement of prayer as an effective and efficient lever to change the way things are, or might otherwise have been, we will seek to authenticate supplicatory and intercessory prayer within the God-given economy of faith and discipleship.

Job laments how:

I cry to you and you do not answer me;
I stand, and you merely look at me.

Job 30:20

Whilst the psalmist pleads:
O my God, I cry by day, but you do not answer;
and by night, but find no rest.

Psalm 22:2

Shakespeare asks whether we are troubling 'deaf heav'n with [our] bootless cries',[2] and that question hangs over us even as we fall, like Lincoln, to our knees in devotion or desperation. To that question we now turn.

Francis Galton was a noted, even notorious, sceptic who came to prominence towards the end of the nineteenth century. He saw evidence-based scientific method as crucial to human progress and flourishing, and was intent upon using such methods to expose the flaws in religious claims to be in touch with reality, not least in relation to what is technically known as impetratory prayer – i.e., aiming at getting things by praying for them.[3] Suppliant, intercessory and petitionary prayer would all fall within this definition. So Galton conducted a statistical enquiry to see if amounts of such prayer resulted in things happening or not.

Galton noted that the crowned heads of Europe were prayed for on a very regular basis, and those prayers were usually for them to be granted long life. But when he compared the longevity of monarchs between 1758 and 1843 he concluded that, when compared to other less prayed for classes of people over the same period, 'the sovereigns are literally the shortest lived of all who have the benefit of affluence . . . the prayer has, therefore, no efficacy'. Furthermore, he noted that insurance companies do not

---

2. Sonnet 29.
3. See Vincent Brümmer, *What Are We Doing When We Pray?*, (SCM, 1984), p.7ff.

give preferential treatment to people who are prayed for on a regular basis when it comes to calculating their premiums.

Scientific method relies on experimentation and evidence gathering in order to verify truth claims in the real world, and it is simply not the case that prayer gets results in the same sense as medical interventions succeed or fail in getting results. Galton believed that he had shown impetratory prayer to be pointless and claims for its efficacy to be fallacious. If he was right, then we would indeed be 'troubling heav'n with bootless cries' whenever we utter a prayer for our own or others' well-being.

The philosophical term for such reliance on scientific testing and verification to establish truth is Positivism, and as a product of the Enlightenment it has dominated many debates about religion in the modern world. When it comes to undermining prayers of petition or intercession, it is simply a matter of accumulating statistical evidence to show how often it fails to deliver the desired results. The influence of Positivism on the modern mind has been extremely pervasive, and God's failure to deliver on perfectly reasonable and heartfelt requests for healing or peace or deliverance from danger has become the most oft-rehearsed challenge to the cogency of petitionary prayer in an age of science and reason.

But it would be a mistake to take Galton's challenge lying down because, quite simply, he was himself mistaken. He was mistaken methodologically because his 'control group' (a very necessary factor in statistical research) was 'those who have the benefit of affluence' whereas, of course, he really needed to compare sovereigns not regularly prayed for with those who were, and this he did not, or even could not, do. Furthermore, members of each group would need to have experienced the same lifestyles and levels of medical care if he were to isolate prayer as a determinative factor in their longevity. However, of more importance is that he was guilty of what is technically known as a category mistake. He assumed that praying for the recovery of someone who is ill is logically the same kind of thing as performing a medical procedure, whereas they are different kinds of activity. Impetratory prayer is first and foremost a matter between the petitioner and God who is believed to have an ongoing interest in the world and its welfare. A medical intervention is a matter between medical practitioners and their patient with the results of that intervention directly measurable and evaluated without the involvement of third parties – divine or otherwise. That is why Ecclesiasticus advises:

> My child, when you are ill, do not delay,
> but pray to the Lord, and he will heal you.
> Give up your faults and direct your hands rightly,
> and cleanse your heart from all sin.
> Offer a sweet-smelling sacrifice, and a memorial
> portion of choice flour,
> and pour oil on your offering,
> as much as you can afford.
> Then give the physician his place,
> for the Lord created him;
> do not let him leave you, for you need him.
> *Ecclesiasticus 38:9-12*

Prayer is one thing; medicine is something else, and although the one may indeed have a direct effect on the other, that is in God's hands, and definitely not the stuff of statistical analysis. In other words, when we reflect on this kind of prayer, we recognise that we are delving into a different category of human experience than can be contained purely by the application of scientific criteria. The categories of experience we describe as spiritual or theological or religious are not in opposition to the scientific and empirically verifiable dimensions of our daily lives, but they are not reducible to those dimensions either. Ecclesiasticus wisely recommends our reliance on both, but that does not mean they are subject to the same tests when it comes to their value and authenticity.

John Wesley wrote a handbook of practical medicine entitled *Primitive Physick* in which he emphasised the importance of relying on remedies that could be proved to work on the basis of scientific experiment – but not to the exclusion of 'that Old, Unfashionable Medicine, Prayer'.[4] He clearly saw these approaches as complementary, but not homogeneous.

So Galton has not disposed of petitionary prayer as a legitimate and worthwhile human endeavour. But he has challenged us to show how such prayer is different from other more statistically measurable activity, and why prayer makes a positive difference even if its results are not as positively verifiable as his experiments seem to demand.[5]

---

4. John Wesley, Preface to *Primitive Physick*, (London, 1747), pp.ix-x & xviii.
5. See F. Galton, 'Statistical Inquiries into the Efficacy of Prayer'. *The Fortnightly Review*, 1 August 1872. Also, S. G. Brush, 'The Prayer Test'. *American Scientist.* 62 (1972) pp.561-563; David Wilkinson, *When I Pray, What Does God Do?*, (Monarch Books, 2015), pp.66-74.

These challenges bring theology and philosophy to the fore, and in as accessible a way as possible, it is those resources we will draw upon to develop a coherent and intellectually sustainable account of what happens when we pray.

Chapter two

Intercessory prayer – a priority and a problem

1. The priority of prayer

The place of prayer as a priority in the Judaeo-Christian tradition is beyond question. Throughout the Bible we encounter people praying and exhorting others to pray. From jubilant praise to sorrowful lamentation, prayer is the medium whereby the bonds of relationship between God and God's people are secured, sometimes severed, but ultimately restored. Adoration, Confession and Thanksgiving feature prominently in the biblical catalogue of prayer, but we also encounter impetratory prayer in the form of petitions and intercessions. One of the most poignant references to the priority of such prayer is found in 1 Samuel 12:23 where Samuel reassures the people, 'Far be it from me that I should sin against the Lord by ceasing to pray for you.'

Like Samuel, prophets and kings in the Hebrew Scriptures are intercessors both for individuals and the nation (see Nehemiah 2:4 and Isaiah 56:7). In the Gospels we set the Lord's Prayer centre stage and note that, being cast in the first person plural, it is essentially an act of intercession. Jesus encourages his disciples to pray for others as well as for themselves (Luke 6:28), and sets an example by his own prayers of intercession (Luke 22:32 and 23:34). This theme is developed most expansively in John (see especially 17:9-26). The Epistles repeatedly stress the importance of praying for one another within the Body of Christ, and Paul goes so far as to urge that 'petitions, intercessions, and thanksgivings be offered for everyone' (1 Timothy 2:1, REB).

David Wilkinson writes about prayer from a decidedly evangelical perspective and devotes himself to an extended study of how prayer features in the Bible. He concludes that:

> The biblical material on how God answers prayer is not straightforward. It does not give a simple model and say this is how you do it in order to get this answer . . . there are parts of the biblical account where we would like to have much more detail, but some of God's ways do remain hidden . . . However, all of the biblical material seems united in one thing – that God has the power to do whatever he likes even if he chooses not to do certain things.[6]

This conclusion is significant because it acknowledges the need for theological and philosophical reflection on the biblical material if we are to get behind the practice of prayer in order to clarify what is actually happening when we pray. The Bible does not provide a clear and definitive account or explanation. Yet, as Wilkinson demonstrates, there is throughout the Bible a clear assumption that prayer, including petitionary and intercessory prayer, is a crucial expression of Judaeo-Christian faith and a key component in corporate and personal piety.

So it comes as no surprise that prayer for the Church, for the world, and especially for those in need, has been at the heart of Christian liturgies from the earliest days, and has

---

6. Wilkinson, *When I Pray, What Does God Do?*, pp.109-110.

been seen as central to the devotional practice of Christians *en famille* or in private. Manuals of devotion provide templates for structuring and organising petitionary prayer,[7] and Orders of Service for public use generally include forms of intercession appropriate to seasons and circumstances. These are necessary because leading intercessions in public worship is not easy, and it is commonplace to parody the efforts of clergy and lay people. James Wood, in his novel *The Book Against God*, is clearly drawing on painful experience when he describes how a vicar

> enjoined his congregation to pray to God for – everything. For the wonderful weather, for the lunch we will soon go and eat, for Muriel's swift recovery, and so on . . . We pray also for the thousands made homeless by the recent flooding in Bangladesh . . . for Dr. Shields, whose cousin was involved in a car accident in Birmingham last Monday, and for Lance and Angela whose son Austin died of leukaemia on Friday.[8]

The temptation to treat the intercessions as a news summary and reprise of local gossip is all too obvious, and it is a shame that books on preaching outnumber books on interceding by a factor of approximately twenty to one. After all, while preaching involves speaking to and with people in God's name, leading intercessions carries the even more important responsibility to speak for those present in enabling the offering up to God of their cares and concerns, hopes and fears.

---

7. See *In His Presence.*
8. James Wood, *The Book Against God* (Vintage, 2004), p.51.

But for our purposes, it is not so much the performance of intercessory prayer which concerns us here as the principles which undergird it. It is at this point in public worship, as in our private devotions, when we find the question pressing itself upon us with ever increasing urgency: what are we doing?

2. The problem with prayer

While the atheist Francis Galton believed that his statistical analysis dealt a fatal blow to the cogency of impetratory prayer, such prayer has also been subject to what might be called 'friendly fire' from a range of theological and philosophical points of view. These have been mainly to do with how the kinds of characteristics we attribute to God – omniscience, omnipotence, changelessness, etc. – can be reconciled with people asking God for certain things to be the case in our world, and expecting things to be so at least partly as a result of such petitions.

So if God is immutable – that is, he cannot change – then presumably he cannot change his mind. That being the case, petitioning God to do something is futile because he is either going to do it or not going to do it, and no amount of prayer can effect a change in what a changeless God has already determined will be the case. Prayer may still have value in terms of its effect on the one who is praying, and so will not be utterly futile, but it cannot have an effect on the course of events which God has already willed to be the case. When the prophet Amos petitioned God for a change of heart in the face of a plague of locusts and an all-consuming fire, we are told that God relented: '"It shall not be," said the Lord.'

(Amos 7:3-6). Yet how can this scenario make sense if God is immutable?

A great deal hangs on the answer to this question. One of the things we treasure most about God's nature is that God is personal, and is therefore capable of a personal relationship with us and others. Such personal relationships are necessarily reactive in the sense that persons interact and thereby each influences what the other thinks or feels or does. It would be difficult to have a personal relationship with a pre-programmed robot which has, in its turn, pre-programmed the future and rendered it immutable. But surely it is the fact that God is personal that controls and ultimately trumps an assertion of absolute immutability. If God is absolutely changeless, then in dealing with God we are effectively dealing with a robot, and how can praying to a robot make any sense at all?

But as a personal God, God is relatively rather than absolutely immutable. For example, as Brümmer puts it, we can trust God to be unchanging when it comes to his character: 'there is never the slightest likelihood that he will ever become fickle or succumb to weakness of will and act out of character'.[9] This is the quality of changelessness to which we appeal when we sing, 'O Thou who changest not, abide with me',[10] and it does not preclude God changing his mind in response to human prayers, for example – indeed, it is precisely the changeless aspects of God's nature that make such changes of mind possible and sometimes necessary. This inevitably provokes further questions about whether and

9. Brümmer, *What Are We Doing When We Pray?*, p.40.
10. H. F. Lyte (1793–1847), 'Abide with me'.

why God seems to act decisively in response to some prayers, but not others, and that is a question to which we shall return. But for now, let us stay with challenges posed to impetratory prayer by God's presumed characteristics.

One such is God's omniscience. If God already knows the future, when we petition God in prayer we are either asking for something which he already knows will be the case or asking for something which he already knows will not be the case, and so prayer is pointless. Again, as with the matter of God's immutability, we can argue (and we will argue!) that impetratory prayer can never be utterly futile because there is positive value in the very fact of asking when contrasted with mere resignation to whatever will be. But at a philosophical level, God's omniscience does seem to blunt the point and purposefulness of our petitions and intercessions, and so needs to be addressed.

One approach to this problem is to locate God in a timeless eternity from which he can know all of history at once and so see all events as they occur – occurring to God simultaneously rather than sequentially. In that case, God is not omniscient in the sense of existing in the present moment and knowing in advance what is going to happen in the future. Past, present and future are known to him without any kind of temporal differentiation so that our prayers, for example, and his response to them, feature in his panorama. In this way, God might be said to know the future, thus honouring his attribute of omniscience, without necessarily determining it.

However, the difficulty with this very elegant solution to our problem is that it effectively makes the idea of change redundant. By definition, change entails moving from one state of affairs in time to another state of affairs in time, while when God sees all events simultaneously, the chance for change to occur is eliminated. Things are as they are in that moment of divine perception, and that is that, so no amount of prayer can actually change anything from God's point of view.

Another approach is to acknowledge that just as God cannot do what cannot logically be done (he cannot make a blue flower which is black), so he cannot know what cannot logically be known. This would include those parts of the future that are yet to be determined, including the prayers we freely choose to make to God on our own behalf or on behalf of others. God's omniscience might be extended to include foreknowledge of what we might do in any possible situation, and that could include our inclination to pray for certain things. But that would still remain part of an indeterminate future which, by logical definition, even an omniscient God could not know because the future in all its detail is logically unknowable.

Of course, this approach seriously qualifies any attribution to God of timeless eternity – what Kierkegaard described as 'the infinite qualitative difference' between the eternal God and God's temporal creation. But even Kierkegaard acknowledged that the Incarnation effectively bridged that difference so that theologically, if not philosophically, there might be a means whereby God's timeless omniscience could graciously accommodate our time-bound petitions.

This must be the case if there is to be any kind of personal relationship between God and his human creation. It must especially be the case if that relationship is predicated upon love as God's essential motivation in making the world and relating to the world he has made. If we can speak of God as relatively immutable, then we can also speak of God's qualified omniscience – qualified not only by the demands of formal logic but also by the demands of a loving relationship between an almighty Creator and his creatures who can thereby approach him in prayer and know that approach to be purposeful.

This leads us seamlessly into another area of philosophical debate when it comes to how what we believe to be God's nature appears to conflict with the practice of impetratory prayer. If God knows what we want, then why does he not simply supply our needs, because surely that is what the assumed goodness of God requires of him? There are two issues at stake here. First of all, as the *Book of Common Prayer* puts it, God is he to whom 'all hearts be open, all desires known and from whom no secrets are hid'. This pulls no punches when it comes to God's total awareness of who we are, what we desire and what is going on in our hearts and minds. Knowing all that, there is clearly no impediment to God responding to our desires if minded to do so, and doing so without the need for further information from us in the form of petitionary or intercessory prayer.

In that sense, God is somewhat in the position of a parent who is fully aware of their child's needs and desires without needing to be asked. There will be many occasions when the parent will endeavour to respond appropriately without needing or waiting to be asked, but good parents will also encourage the child to express their needs and desires from time to time, because that is how positive relationships mature over time in a spirit of mutual understanding and reciprocity. Likewise, God routinely makes provision for our needs and fulfils our desires in appropriate ways without waiting upon our supplications. However, making our requests known to God in prayer is necessary to a mature relationship with God, and avoids any risk of God bypassing our will in order to impose his will on us or manipulate us into a state of subservient acquiescence. God does not need to have our will made known to him, but he desires to have a personal and loving relationship with us, and so he is content to temper his power to the offering of our prayers.

So it is not only God's immutability and omniscience which are subject to the requirements of a loving and reciprocal relationship with his people. God's omnipotence is also conditioned by such requirements so that the power of love prevails over the exercise of divine fiat.[11]

The second issue at stake here is a bit more tricky. It takes us into the vexed question of how the exercise of God's goodness can be thought to depend in any sense on what we may or may not ask for ourselves or, more crucially, for other people. This in its turn takes us into debates about the relationship between good and evil in the world, and how the existence of evil can be reconciled with belief in a God of love.

If it is the case that God has the power to do good by us and others but voluntarily makes the exercise of that power conditional upon our petitions and intercessions so that evil may at least sometimes prevail consequent upon the poverty of our prayers, then is his goodness not thereby compromised?

11. See T. J. Gorringe, *God's Theatre: A Theology of Providence* (SCM, 1991), p.94.

He knows what is best but defers to our often inappropriate or inadequate supplications in the interests of keeping his relationship with us on an even keel. Would not a parent be prepared to put that relationship at risk in the interests of their children's well-being? On balance, we believe they would, so why should a good God be any different? In other words, can we sustain the case for a self-limiting God in the face of such evil in the world as our prayers, be they ever so well intended and articulated, can never hope to encompass?

Against such a background, Samuel's 'Far be it from me that I should sin against the Lord by ceasing to pray for you' takes on an overwhelming significance. Sometimes we might feel during a church service that the person leading intercessions is asking us to take all the burdens of the world onto our shoulders simultaneously, and if God acting for good in relation to all those situations does actually depend upon us asking him to do so, then that is surely a burden we cannot, and so should not be asked to, bear. As Helen Oppenheimer put it, 'What is hard to believe in is a God who is supposed to withhold his favour from some apparently worthy person or cause for whom nobody has happened to intercede.'[12]

One way forward with respect to this challenge is to accept that God is indeed the primary cause behind all that happens in the world, but his agency takes effect by means of secondary causes. This approach is adopted by Brümmer,[13] and it is closely associated with the concept of 'double agency' promoted by Austin Farrer. We shall major on this concept in

---

12. Helen Oppenhemer, 'Petitionary Prayer', in *Theology* 73 (1970), p.57.
13. Brümmer, *What Are We Doing When We Pray?*, p.57.

a later chapter (chapter 3, section 4 'Free will conscripted'), but for now we find Brümmer puts the case clearly enough:

> If the 'double agency' theory holds, then intercession is a prayer in which the person who prays both asks God to act on behalf of the person or cause for whom he intercedes, and also makes himself available as secondary cause through whom God could act in answering the prayer. Intercession . . . involves both God and the petitioner as partners in realising what is being asked.[14]

For a biblical example, we can cite the celebrated case of King Hezekiah's boil. According to Isaiah 38 and 2 Kings 20, the king prayed for himself while Isaiah the prophet applied a poultice of figs to the boil that he might recover – and he did! We may ask by what means was the healing achieved? Was it by prayer or poultice, or by a combination of both? Probably the latter, so that the interdependence between prayer and action is illustrated to dramatic effect.[15]

The upshot of all this is that just as we have argued for God's self-limiting love in relation to his omniscience, omnipotence and immutability, so we need now to assert the need for some self-limitation on the part of the petitioner. We should only ask God for those things for which we are ourselves prepared to act to help bring about. We cannot use prayers as a way of shunting on to God responsibilities which we can and should see as

---

14. Brümmer, *What Are We Doing When We Pray?*, p.57.
15. See Michael E. W. Thompson, 'What happens when we pray – a contribution from the Old Testament', *Expository Times*, August 2003, p.370.

placing obligations upon us to act in ways appropriate to our circumstances and capacities. As Ian Ramsey put it:

> If those conditions hold, we are more likely to pray with integrity than if we think of the answer of God as the message of an answering machine, or the kind of message which comes out of a slot-machine which tells us our weight and our fortune.[16]

Peter Baelz is even more astringent:

> To turn to God without at the same time doing all that we can ourselves to bring about what we pray for is . . . idolatrous. For it puts in the place of the true God, who has revealed himself in and through the way the world goes, a false God of our own imagining.[17]

The question still remains as to whether intercessory prayer is itself an action within the terms of 'double agency' theory. There are individuals and communities who devote themselves to intercession for the peace of the world, and for people in need, who are not in a position to act as agents in effecting answers to those prayers. Are they simply uttering 'bootless cries' or, even worse, acting idolatrously? When William Temple said, 'When I pray, coincidences happen'. he seemed to endorse a direct causal link between his prayers and subsequent events even if, or especially when, he was not directly implicated in those events.

This raises all sorts of questions about how God is involved in the world, and we will confront those head on in chapter

---

16. Ian T. Ramsey, *Our Understanding of Prayer* (SPCK, 1971) pp.21-22.
17. P. Baelz, *Does God Answer Prayer?* (Darton, Longman and Todd, 1982), pp.43-44.

three. Let us assume for now that intercessions do impact on what happens, and that the absence of such prayers also has an effect. Can it be that intercessions offered by those unable for good reasons to be actively involved in helping to bring about the desired effects are ruled out of order by a benevolent God? Surely this is where the doctrine of intentionality kicks in. This notion has a long pedigree in Christian theology, and although it has no doubt been used from time to time as a get-out clause by those seeking to absolve themselves from things they have not done which they ought to have done, still it reflects those qualities of mercy and grace which we associate with God's goodness and loving kindness. If members of religious communities, or housebound people, take it upon themselves to intercede for the needs of the world, and would be active in helping to address those needs if they were not disabled from doing so, then those prayers must be counted to them for righteousness. They would act if they could, so their intentions are good, and given their circumstances it is the act of intercession itself which must stand as their offering to God to be placed at God's disposal.[18]

So one way in which the goodness of God can be reconciled with his reliance on our prayers to affect future events is that such supplication, when rightly and properly motivated, encourages action in support of those prayers. Furthermore, when such prayers are offered communally, as is the case during public worship, they can stimulate collective action in support of the causes for which God's agency, in cooperation with our own, has been invoked. Finally, prayers offered for oneself or others in circumstances

18. See Ramsey, *Our Understanding of Prayer*, p.22.

where our own agency is compromised can be believed to be positively received into God's agency on the basis of one's intention to act if circumstances were otherwise. To use prayer as a way of transferring on to God responsibilities we should shoulder ourselves is a must to avoid. But if, as Richard Swinburne argues, by requiring petitionary and intercessory prayer in some cases, God gives us more responsibility for the well-being of ourselves and others than would otherwise be the case, then that is entirely consistent with belief in God's goodness.[19]

Yet a further way in which we must exercise some self-discipline is in relation to the things about which and for which we pray. God could not be described as good and benevolent if he were simply to assent to whatever we asked without reference to his own nature and purposes in creating and sustaining the world. This means that if we pray for what is contrary to God's nature, we undermine the personal relationship God seeks to establish with us. That relationship is predicated upon a spirit of cooperation, and so acquainting ourselves as best we can with what it is God wills for the world is crucial to praying with integrity. As the *Common Worship* Collect for the Tenth Sunday after Trinity puts it:

> Let your merciful ears, O Lord, be open to the prayers of your humble servants; and that they may obtain their petitions make them to ask such things as shall please you; Through Jesus Christ your Son our Lord.

---

19. Richard Swinburne, *Providence and the Problem of Evil* (Oxford University Press, 1998).

For Christians, it is above all through the self-giving of himself in Jesus that we access God's nature. We seek to have the mind of Christ (1 Corinthians 2:16), and to bring that perspective to bear on how we pray and for what we pray. The Gospels contain a rich seam of teaching by Jesus about prayer (e.g. Luke 11:1-13), and as Alan Richardson has expressed it:

> If our communion with God is even a faltering reflection of Jesus' own intimate sonship, we shall not be able to prevent ourselves from bringing to our heavenly Father all the concerns which press upon us. If we have the Spirit of Jesus in us, these concerns will be for others rather than for ourselves; but our own personal griefs and problems will, quite naturally, not be excluded from our speaking with God.[20]

This offers us an expansive range of possibilities when it comes to our supplications, but it does not allow us to trespass beyond the virtues and values of the kingdom of God for which Jesus, above all, taught us to pray. When we align our prayers with what we believe to be the fundamental trajectory of God's will for 'life, and life in all its fullness' (John 10:10, REB), then we can safely say that, by entrusting to us the privilege of offering our petitions and intercessions, God's goodness has been given yet another medium whereby it can be recognised and celebrated.

Conclusion

That prayer is a priority for Christians is universally acknowledged, but the problems posed by impetratory

---

20. Alan Richardson, *A New Dictionary of Christian Theology* (SCM, 1983), p.458.

prayer are not so readily addressed. Whether from the intellectual high ground claimed by scientific positivists and secular rationalists, or from within the community of faith itself through proponents of philosophical theology, the provenance and plausibility of such prayers has been under severe scrutiny. This is all to the good, quite simply because 'it is a fearful thing to fall into the hands of the living God'. We do well to ensure as best we can that when we make our supplications unto God we are not guilty of idolatry, illogicality, irresponsibility or mere wishful thinking!

However, I hope I have shown how these critiques of impetratory prayer have failed to undermine the cogency and coherence of a practice which goes to the heart of our relationship with God. Indeed, the very nature of a personal relationship has been central to our argument that God's attributes as immutable, omniscient, omnipotent and good, and our responsibilities as cooperators with God as revealed to us in Jesus Christ, are essentially subject to the requirements of a healthy and maturing relationship between God and God's people. Some degree of self-limitation is required by both the one who offers and the one who receives prayers of petition and intercession, and it is this willingness on the part of Godself and oneself that is the very essence of a loving relationship and the key to the peculiarity and credibility of prayers for ourselves, for others and for a world entrusted to our care.

We have drawn on the analogy of personal relationships to argue that although an omniscient and omnipotent God could act as Creator in ways that take no account of our prayers, the quality of such a relationship between us and God is enriched by God's openness to our desires and requests, whether on our own behalf or on behalf of others. Employers, managers and head teachers who operate an open-door policy are generally credited with fostering better relationships with their staff than those who give no opportunity for concerns and suggestions to be shared with them. Whether or not those concerns and suggestions are acted upon clearly matters, but might matter less than the fact that they have been given the chance to be heard. So God operating an open-ears policy with respect to our petitions and intercessions likewise fosters better relationships with his people than would be the case if he were always to act without any sense of their having been heard. It might be argued that a prayer offered is a prayer received, and a prayer received is a prayer answered, and that is enough. As F. B. Meyer put it, 'The greatest tragedy in life is not unanswered prayer, but unoffered prayer.'[21] Whether or not our prayers impact directly upon what an all-knowing and all-powerful deity actually does in the world, the very fact of having made all our desires known, and knowing ourselves to have been heard, is sufficient for us – and we look no further to justify our supplications.

However, we cannot set aside scriptural testimony to the effect that such prayers are not only heard but are answered in ways that go beyond being simply received. Jesus' teaching on prayer confirms that those who ask, receive (Luke 11:10), and impetratory prayer with the expectation of a response has been at the heart of Christian faith and practice ever since. So we shall not rest content with simply being heard, gratifying

---

21. F. B. Meyer, quoted in Philip Yancey, *Prayer: Does It Make Any Difference?* (Hodder & Stoughton, 2006), p.275.

though that is to know. We must explore further what is entailed by the belief that prayers can be related directly to what happens in the world by God's hand – and we must examine why it might be that some prayers are answered in the terms in which they have been offered, and some are not.

Key to such inquiry must be how we understand God's action in the world. This will take us into the tension between God's sovereignty and human freedom, and the ways in which our approach to petititonary and intercessory prayer are impacted by that tension. To such an inquiry we now turn.

Chapter three

God's sovereignty and our freedom – a spectrum of possibilities

> We have to conceive how transcendent divine activity can be diversely structured to relate to specific worldly occurrences with initiative and sovereignty, without compromising divine love or demands of creaturely freedom, and without making nonsense of modern world views.[22]

With admirable concision, Vernon White summarises the challenge which faces us when we seek to define and describe how God can be active in the world. Note that the problems are not caused by God's attributes of omnipotence, omniscience, etc. We have seen how, although these attributes must pertain to God, limiting himself in respect of those attributes does not negate them or his divine integrity. In fact, God as personal, and therefore relational, requires such self-limitation as an expression of his love and goodness.

However, if God is active in the world in such a way as to respond to our prayers in relation to what goes on in the world, then there are implications for God's sovereignty on the one hand, and human freedom on the other. This tension has been at the heart of philosophical theology since the days of Origen, Irenaeus and Augustine. As Vernon White indicates,

---

22. Vernon White, *The Fall of a Sparrow: A concept of special divine action* (Paternoster, 1985), p.96.

it is a tension which has acquired even greater import in an age when theological claims must answer at the bar of reason and science rather than relying on revelation and tradition as the only arbiters of acceptable beliefs and practices.

In this chapter we will focus first of all on those approaches to God's action in the world which major on God's sovereign power and will, and access the implications for petitionary and intercessory prayer. Then we will attend to those approaches which prioritise human freedom. This will result in a spectrum of possibilities which we might recognise as inclusive of much that we ourselves experience in relation to impetratory prayer, and which can help us to understand and interpret the ways in which we and others pray corporately and privately. We may conclude that just one point on this spectrum satisfies us, and there we stand! On the other hand, we may find some truth to treasure at all or several points on the spectrum so that our practice of prayer is extended and enriched. Either way, the journey will have been worthwhile.

1. Sovereignty supreme

So how might we 'conceive how transcendent divine activity can be diversely structured to relate to specific worldly occurrences with initiative and sovereignty'? One answer is to simply assert that everything that has happened, that is happening and that will happen in the future has been predetermined by God, whose sovereign status negates any possibility of events being subject to creaturely influences or contingencies. God cannot be somewhat sovereign, or sovereign to a certain extent. On this account, divine sovereignty must be absolute and beyond the constraints of possibility, probability or provisionality. To protect God's absolute sovereignty, it is likely that theologians will be drawn to notions of predetermination or even to predestination as the only means to prevent what is created from compromising the will and purpose of the Creator.

This kind of approach is predicated on God as analogous to the sole author, drafter, director and producer of an animation film. He writes the script, draws the characters and their contexts, sequences the action and signs off the final version. Once the finished product is in the can, that is that. Nothing and no one can change what is a complete and self-contained piece of creative art. So God can be conceived to be the sole author, director and producer of all that has been, is and is to come. He has signed off on Creation as a complete and self-contained work which is unfolding in accordance with a predetermined trajectory towards a foregone conclusion. In a sense, this approach avoids issues to do with the changelessness of God by asserting the changelessness of Creation. Giving the creature any sort of potential to order differently what has already been predetermined by the Creator would impact negatively on the Creator's absolute power and sovereignty, and is to be avoided at all costs . . . and the costs are very great indeed.

First of all, there is no room in such a scenario for creaturely freedom. Just as a cartoon character has no will of its own to influence the animator, so God's creatures, human or otherwise, have no power to influence present or future eventualities. God's absolute sovereignty is bought at the price of everyone's and everything's absolute impotence. Thomas Hardy saw life as determined by fate: 'that ingenious machinery contrived by the gods for reducing human possibilities of amelioration to a minimum'.[23] This negates the possibility of any kind of meaningful relationship between creature and creator apart from one of unilateral manipulation. Needless to say, any talk of a loving relationship is ruled out by the inability of creatures to love the creator unless the creator has pre-programmed them to do so, and what is the worth of a love manipulated in such a way?

Of course, such an absolutist approach to God's sovereignty impacts decisively on the practice of prayer. Whether we are talking about adoration, confession, thanksgiving or supplication, we are describing something which God has already programmed into what we and others do in our day-to-day lives, and even our heartfelt desire to pray is the outworking of God's will and not our own. When we pray, 'Thy will be done', we might be colluding with a predeterminist model of God's action in the world – a brand of resignation or fatalism so that what will be, will be.

However, this phrase in the Lord's Prayer is in fact intended to imply the fuller plea of Jesus in Gethsemane: 'Not my will, but thine be done' (Mark 14:36, my translation). He explicitly refers to his own will on the clear understanding that he has one, and that it is in some sense independent of God's will. Furthermore, nothing in the Gospels suggests that in this respect Jesus was different from us. Having a will of his own is, rather, a sign of Jesus' humanity rather than an indicator of Christological distinctiveness. If the petition

---

23. Quoted in Claire Tomalin, *Thomas Hardy – the time-torn man* (Penguin, 2007), p.218.

'Thy will be done' in the Lord's Prayer does exclude our will from the taxonomy of prayer, it may as well stop at that. But the fact that this model prayer does go on to make petitions for daily bread, forgiveness of sins and deliverance from evil underscores the belief that not only God's will but our will is in play when we pray, and our will is at least to some extent free and not negated by a predeterminist account of divine providence. As Peter Baelz puts it:

> A merely passive 'Thy will be done' may be the expression of submission to God, but it involves a partial withdrawal of ourselves. We resign ourselves and give in to God rather than wrestle with him until day breaks (cf. Genesis 32:24).[24]

2. Sovereignty suspended

It is tempting to see the predeterminist approach as akin to the movement of thought known as Deism. This movement came to the fore as an attempt to honour Vernon White's plea not 'to make nonsense of modern world views' when it comes to how we conceive God's action in the world. Newtonian mechanics combined with Enlightenment rationalism and empiricism to challenge any kind of supernatural interference with the consistently smooth and predictable functioning of the laws of nature. It belongs largely to the seventeenth and eighteenth centuries and, as a term, Deism covers a wide spectrum of ideas and personalities. But by and large it can be said that rather than major on God as predetermining what happens in the world, Deists asserted the determinative character of natural order so that while God may have set

---

24. Baelz, *Does God Answer Prayer?*, p.41.

that order in motion and prescribed natural laws to govern it, he cannot be thought of as intervening in the operation of those laws by means of miracles, revelations, incarnations or anything else.

As Michael Goulder famously commented, 'the deistic God was sacked in the nineteenth century for doing no work',[25] and this was clearly a stepping stone on the way to what has become known as New Atheism. For our purposes, suffice it to say that, in relation to the practice of prayer, it did not reduce it to a predetermined activity in a predetermined universe. Rather, it limited the possible scope and potential efficacy of prayer to petitions and outcomes consistent with the laws of nature – a perspective on prayer which, as we shall see, has persisted long after Deism ran its course.

While we have found much to criticise in predeterminism, and we have seen the existence and importance of free will as key to those criticisms, still we must acknowledge the priority placed on God's sovereignty and beware lest our defence of free will compromise dimensions of what it means for God to be God. The concept of God intervening in the world as assumed by Scripture, and confirmed in the experience of countless people down the centuries, must be taken seriously and not be sacrificed on the altar of modern philosophical and scientific sensibilities. Indeed, relatively recent developments in the discipline of sub-atomic physics suggest that the notions of a closed universe based on the mechanistic certainties of Newtonian physics can no longer be considered normative.

David Wilkinson's informed and detailed account of recent scientific studies in particle physics and chaos theory

---

25. M. Goulder & J. Hick, *Why Believe in God?* (SCM, 1974), p.89.

concludes that attacks on the effectiveness of impetratory prayer have generally relied on belief in a closed mechanistic universe, and the new science poses severe challenges to such objections. He does not go so far as to suggest that the new physics provides solid scientific support for miracles or specific divine interventions in response to our prayers, but such paradigm shifts in the philosophy of science should cause us to question claims that science has rendered prayer redundant by virtue of having explained it away.[26] That being the case, we must turn to consider how God's sovereignty can be established on the basis of what we generally identify as miracles – i.e., God at least occasionally intervening to overrule or override the laws of nature, and possibly doing so in direct response to impetratory prayers.

3. Sovereignty sometimes

What is a miracle? It could be defined as an action or event that apparently violates the accepted course of nature. In one sense this is too a strong a definition because the words 'miracle' and 'miraculous' have come to denote anything which is remarkable and out of the ordinary but not necessarily in violation of any law of nature – so David Beckham's ability to bend a ball from a free kick is 'miraculous'.

On the other hand, our definition is too weak because it fails to take account of the agent through whom the miracle is done and the belief system to which they relate. So Jesus' healings in the Gospels echo those performed by many itinerant healers at that time, but are deemed miraculous precisely because they are performed by the Son

26. Yancey, *Prayer: Does It Make Any Difference?*, p.72.

of God and are signs of the in-breaking of God's kingdom. Miracles separated from their transcendent and supernatural moorings are reduced to mere magic. Whether for Christians those moorings relate to the Christ event, to the sacramental ministrations of the Church or to the ongoing activity of the Holy Spirit, the key point is that they are of God, and have significance only insofar as God is their originator and guarantor.

It is for this reason that many religious believers find it so easy to discount the scepticism of those whose secularist presuppositions blind them to a dimension of reality perceived only through the eyes of faith. But such a retreat into fideism is premature. Surely we must be prepared to take our beliefs to the bar of rational and scientific criticism and be bold in the face of such scrutiny. There are many reasons why the idea of miracles is problematic, and we need to address them with due regard to their seriousness – not least when it is claimed that miracles can be, and often are, answers to prayer.

It was under the influence of the seventeenth-century philosopher Benedict de Spinoza that the burden of proof shifted when it came to the authenticity of miracles. Up until then miracles were generally accepted as genuine violations of the laws of nature, and the case for Christianity as true and verifiable largely rested on this acceptance. Indeed, it is arguable that such events as the crossing of the Red Sea in Exodus were described in increasingly miraculous terms as the story was told and retold over time. An extraordinarily favourable set of weather conditions on the day in question morphed into a narrative suffused with miraculous effects, precisely to substantiate belief in the sovereign power of God in support of his chosen people. Such belief could be justified on account of the favourable but entirely natural conditions on the day, but gilding the account with supernatural details rendered it even more credible as proof of God's providence. Some would say that miracle stories in the New Testament went through a similar process of elaboration to enhance what Pooh Bah in *The Mikado* might describe as 'an otherwise dull and unconvincing narrative'.

Certainly up until the time of Spinoza there would have been little doubt that evidence of the miraculous helped rather than hindered Christianity's claim to be true and historically validated. But as modernity took its course, so appeals to the miraculous became less and less effective in the work of apologetics and evangelism – and would be experienced by many as embarrassing and counterproductive. Interpreting uncommonly propitious weather conditions such as those experienced during the evacuation at Dunkirk in 1941 as evidence of God's providence retains an allure. But this would be seen more as a 'weak' miracle (i.e., remarkable and momentous but still within the laws of nature) rather than a 'strong' miracle (i.e., caused by circumstances unrelated to the laws of nature). It is now for Christians to prove the authenticity of miracles rather than miracles proving the authenticity of Christian beliefs.

The Scottish philosopher David Hume challenged the view that testimony to any kind of miracle amounted to a probability, let alone a proof. Others, in the wake of the Enlightenment, were adamant that claims for a miracle would always fail the tests of rationalism and empiricism. If an event presents as miraculous, it is best to assume that it has a perfectly natural causal explanation, even if we do not yet know exactly what it is.

However, Christians have not been slow to counter what, in the western world at least, is the prevailing mood of scepticism and scientific reductionism. Accounts of 'strong' miracles continue to circulate around the shrine at Lourdes, and in many Pentecostal and Charismatic communities. These claims might be said to simply ignore the Enlightenment, with a positive determination 'to make nonsense of modern world views' by appeals to revelation, tradition and spiritual experience as the ultimate arbiters of truth and authenticity. This approach has its attraction. After all, why should rationalism and empiricism rule the roost when we all know that neither reason nor science can do full explanatory justice to many of the most important emotional, aesthetic and spiritual experiences which characterise our everyday lives? Quite so, but we are challenged to love the Lord our God with all our mind as well as with all our heart, soul and strength (Mark 12:30). The fact of the matter is that the way in which we now make sense of the world around us does depend upon the consistency of logical reasoning and the reliability of natural laws. Insofar as miracles are at odds with such consistency and reliability, we do have to take that seriously and acknowledge that a high hurdle has been placed in the way of their acceptance as proofs of divine providence and answers to prayer.

There is much to be said for ways in which modern theologians have nuanced Christian accounts of the miraculous in recent decades. They do so in various ways, ranging from seeing miracle stories as more mythical than historical to seeing them as essentially having theological and spiritual import with their historical basis being only of secondary significance. In other words, they incline away from 'strong' versions of what might count as miracles, and if they are prepared to countenance miracles at all it is in the weaker sense of remarkable events subject to extraordinary but still natural causes. This is understandable in response to the highly critical stance towards miracles adopted by most post-Enlightenment philosophers, but it also reflects a shift towards the free will end of the sovereignty–free will spectrum.

It is curious that post-modern philosophers and scientists are increasingly inclined towards the possibility of 'strong' miracles (the former because of perceived flaws in the sceptics' case, and the latter because of the vagaries of sub-atomic particle physics). Yet theologians are less attracted to this trend as essential to religious belief. They might well agree that God can perform such miracles, and that he may indeed have done so especially as part of the ministry of Jesus and the early Church. To that extent, God's sovereignty is acknowledged and affirmed. But there remains a concern as to whether such 'strong' miracles entail interventions in the natural order such as to undermine genuine freedom and, therefore, to compromise God's loving purposes predicated on his gift of free will to his human creatures, and our freely willed response of love in return. Those who maintain the centrality of such miracles in the economy of God do so because God's sovereignty matters most. They believe that if we are not to go down the predeterminist route, then occasional divine interventions in the form of 'strong' miracles are the next best thing.

However, there is a price to be paid insofar as the possibility, let alone the probability, of God intervening threatens the autonomy of our freely willed decisions and actions. Are we really free to decide to do something and then do it if at any point God might overrule the laws of nature and thereby overrule our will and purpose? True, the outcome will almost certainly be better than if matters had been left to run their course, but our freedom will have taken a knock, and our relationship with God will have become significantly less reciprocal.

Here we capture echoes of our earlier consideration of God's attribute of omnipotence and its implications for petitionary and intercessory prayer. When there is a tension between God's power and God's love, it is not a case of one cancelling out the other. Is God Power without Love, or Love without Power? This is another way of expressing the challenge posed as key to the problem of evil – if God wants to prevent evil but cannot, then he is not all-powerful; if God can prevent evil but does not, then he is not all-loving. But what if God is, in fact, Power in Love with the world? God's power is then subject to self-limitation for the sake of securing and safeguarding the necessary conditions for a free and reciprocal relationship of love between us and our creator. Philip Yancey describes this as 'God's style of restraint out of respect for human freedom'.[27]

---

27. Philip Yancey, Prayer: *Does it make any difference?* (Hodder & Stoughton, 2006), p.72.

Perhaps this goes some way towards meeting the challenge of so-called unanswered prayer, especially if such prayer is for God to perform a 'strong' miracle. It is natural for us to pray thus from time to time, and it is no part of my purpose in these pages to discourage or discount such prayers. But we must ask ourselves whether we are primarily seeking to tap into God's power, or whether we are casting our cares and concerns on to God's love when we pray for a miracle. If the former, then the caveat, 'Be careful what you pray for,' kicks in. We are asking God to relate to our world in ways which are difficult to reconcile with the requirements of a truly loving relationship. On the other hand, such prayers offered with an eye to the outworking of God's love as the most wholesome expression of God's power ensures that God's sovereignty is appropriately tempered by our freedom.

It is here that we confront what can be described as the callous insensitivity of those who link apparently unanswered prayer to the petitioner's lack of faith. The fact that someone has not recovered from an illness, notwithstanding their prayers and those offered on their behalf, is explained as a failure to truly believe that God is equal to the task. Lack of faith in God's power disrupts the power supply and there is no miraculous cure. Of course, the New Testament will be cited in support of this view – faith strong enough to move mountains, etc. – but at its core this analysis misses the point. The faith of which Jesus speaks, and which he enjoins upon us, is not faith in God's power to intervene, but faith in God's love in the service of which he disposes his power that his will may be done. Yancey describes how a pastor in his church

would sometimes offer a time for people to come to the front
for prayer:

> The worst thing that can happen to you is that you will
> have an experience of being profoundly loved. That's
> not so bad, is it? And you might just hear the Master's
> voice, 'Your faith has made you whole. Go in peace
> freed from your suffering.'[28]

The faith in question is faith in God's love, and it is only
about faith in God's power insofar as it is God's power in love
with the world. Perhaps it is the difference between what the
Romans called *auctoritas* (the power to inspire) and *potestas*
(the power to compel).

4. Free will conscripted

Now, even if this is accepted, we are still left to wonder about
the appropriateness and provenance of prayers which are not
invoking 'strong' miracles but are still petitioning God to
act through natural processes, and particularly through the
decisions and actions of human agents. This is an attractive
option for those wanting to avoid making nonsense of
modern world views on the one hand, and to strike an
appropriate balance between God's sovereignty and our
freedom on the other. Rather than petitioning God to
intervene directly in a particular situation, we pray, for
example, for doctors, aid agencies or politicians to be effective
in preventing harm or responding when the well-being of
ourselves or others is at risk. These are prayers for what are
called 'weak' miracles, with particular reference to our own

---

28. Yancey, *Prayer: Does It Make Any Difference?*, pp.255-256.

and/or others' potential to make a difference and so effect answers to prayers.

This embrace of 'weak' miracles can be further subdivided into strong and weak versions. The stronger version postulates God's direct influence on human agents as the means whereby prayers might be answered. We pray for God to use the skill of doctors or agriculturalists or aid workers to help in times of sickness, famine or earthquake. This entails a degree of 'double agency' whereby both our will and God's will are at work, and that in one of two ways. The first possibility is that while on the face of it human agents are active in relation to a particular situation for which prayers have been offered, God is at work inspiring, guiding and enabling those actions so that not one but two agencies are operative – one divine and one human.

It is indeed the case that Christian discipleship entails putting ourselves, our gifts, our skills and our opportunities at God's disposal. We sing, 'Make me a channel of your peace', and thereby put ourselves at God's service for the doing of his will. But it is important to remember that this must be a voluntary offering on our part. If our actions are directly manipulated by God to achieve his purposes, then we become too much like puppets in his hands and our apparent freedom is in fact an illusion. This version of double agency is strong on God's sovereignty, but it is more about *potestas* than *auctoritas*, and there is little to be seen of human freedom in such a scenario.

However, a second possibility promises to keep our free will more in balance with God's sovereignty. Imagine a weaver of carpets at work with his assistants. They are one side of the vertical loom passing threads through the loom for the master to weave into a beautiful pattern. They do not have a complete sense of how the finished product is intended to look, but the master does, and his skill is to take whatever they give him and to weave their threads into the pattern he has in mind. Here there is no coercion on the part of the master carpet weaver as the assistants are free to pass through the threads of their choosing, but the outcome is in accordance with his will.

This looks like a promising analogy when it comes to how we understand the outworking of double agency in relation to our human actions in general, and our impetratory prayers in particular. We ask God to take the actions of ourselves and others and weave them into a pattern in accordance with his perfect will. Our actions are freely chosen, and there is no question of God manipulating what we do. He exercises sovereignty by what he does with our offerings, and does so at no cost to our freedom. But is that actually the case? Frances Ridley Havergal's hymn 'Take my life, and let it be consecrated, Lord, to thee' seems to capture this dynamic of double agency to perfection:

Take my intellect, and use
every power as thou shalt choose.

All very well, but the rub comes in the next verse:

Take my will, and make it thine:
it shall be no longer mine.

However affecting the scene, and however attractive the analogy, the carpet weaver's *modus operandi* does not really help us. For sure, we are not being manipulated like puppets, but insofar as we have freedom in our acting and praying, it is only up to a point. We are free to provide ingredients for the final pattern of events, but we have no part to play in fashioning that pattern, so that once again, our freedom is compromised, as is our ability to love God with all our heart, soul, mind and strength. Yet God's readiness to limit himself to working only with the raw materials we provide as human agents is testimony to his 'restraint out of respect for human freedom', and that is why this version of the 'double agency' approach stands as a positive, although still inadequate, account of what we are doing when we pray.

This inadequacy can be met most effectively by majoring on God's love in choosing the most freedom enhancing way of acting in the world. For, as C. S. Lewis puts it:

> He seems to do nothing of Himself which He can possibly delegate to His creatures. He commands us to do slowly and blunderingly what He could do perfectly in the twinkling of an eye. He allows us to neglect what He would have us do, or to fail. Perhaps we do not fully realize the problem, so to call it, of enabling finite free wills to co-exist with Omnipotence. It seems to involve at every moment almost a sort of divine abdication . . . He will do nothing simply of Himself which can be done by creatures.[29]

Whether we call it delegation or abdication, God chooses to honour our freedom by entrusting to us the outworking of his will and purpose. He does this in two ways. First of

---

29. C. S. Lewis, *The World's Last Night* (New York, 1960), p.9, and quoted in Yancey, *Prayer: Does it make any difference?* p.134.

all, by giving us the resources of revelation, tradition, reason and spiritual experience, in light of which we can have the wisdom to know what is right and the courage to do it. By immersing ourselves in God's world and will, we are enabled to respond to his love for us by showing and sharing that love in our words and deeds – including our prayers and our actions in support of our prayers. If we follow St Augustine's advice to love God then do what we like, what we like to do will be as close as we can get to what God wills to be done.

Secondly, he gives us the freedom through our petitions and intercessions to place on record, as it were, our hopes and fears, our desires, and even our demands for the world around us as the future unfolds before us. Ultimately, God's sovereignty requires that how things go in the world accords with his will, culminating in the realisation of his plan and purpose for all he has made. Like a planner commissioned to build a new town, God could simply dictate terms on the principle that he knows best and his creatures must simply accept that this is how things have to be. But a wise town planner will most likely consult with residents and invite them to express what it is they most want from the life they will live in his creation. Not all their wishes can be granted, as some will be incompatible with the planner's overall purpose, or they will be impractical given the range of considerations attached to a project of this kind. And, of course, different requests from different people will cancel each other out. By no means least, it remains true that no one really feels consulted unless their view has prevailed! But being asked to contribute in such a way is a gracious and generous gesture, and we are justified in believing that God will be more likely to act in such a way rather than otherwise. In other words, God wills to see us as partners in his work of creation and providential care.

Here we have reached a crucial stage in our journey along the spectrum of possibilities pertaining to the practice of impetratory prayer. A tipping point has been reached with God's self-limitation of power, and his determination to partner with us as free agents in the providential ordering of existence, shifting the emphasis towards the free will end of the spectrum. As Wilkinson puts it, 'God is omnipotent but limits his own power to give freedom.'[30] God's sovereignty is more a matter of delegation than dictation. Consequently, an increasing burden of responsibility is borne by the persons praying so as to ensure that what they pray for is theologically appropriate, ethically considered and consistent with the flourishing of freedom.

In his short but typically penetrating pamphlet, *Our Understanding of Prayer*, Bishop Ian Ramsey leaves us in no doubt that while we may sometimes find ourselves in such desperate straits that we simply invoke God's power to intervene and save us, the real authenticity and integrity of impetratory prayer relies on our readiness to be a party to the answer and a partner with God in delivering it:

There is an old phrase often used in appeal brochures, 'We want your prayers and your money'. This phrase, while making a point, can be very misleading. For in this context prayers would not be prayers unless the gift of money was part of the one action, and a gift

---

30. Wilkinson, *When I Pray, What Does God Do?*, p.174. See also J. C. Polkinhorne, *Science and Providence* (SPCK, 1989), pp.70-71.

of money is no Christian dedication unless it is an outreach pointing back to a moment of vision in prayer. To suggest, therefore, that praying and giving can be thought of as two separable activities is to misunderstand both. But to see them as inextricably linked is the way in which secularity and spirituality come together as one. For prayer without any practical support or secular expression is empty, as secularity without prayer is unredeemed. Action and prayer are two expressions of one situation; in praying and doing each fulfils the other. The deepest spirituality and the most active participation are one.[31]

Note that Ramsey is not saying that our active participation in following through on our prayers is merely optional or desirable. It is absolutely necessary because without it prayer is not prayer at all, and is akin to thinking of the answer of God as 'the message of an answering machine, or the kind of message which comes out of a slot-machine which tells us our weight and our fortune'.[32] As Peter Baelz concludes, 'Praying is not a substitute for doing, nor is doing a substitute for praying.'[33]

5. Free will comforted

There is a popular variation on the view that God intervenes to answer prayers by using human agency. It stops short of imputing direct divine intervention in the shape of doctors'

---

31. I. T. Ramsey, *Our Understanding of Prayer*, pp.22-23.
32. Ramsey, *Our Understanding of Prayer*, pp.21-22.
33. Baelz, *Does God Answer Prayer?* p.43.

hands, or aid workers' resources being used by God to act for him in relieving sickness or famine. Rather, it focuses more on the mindset of human agents so that prayer changes their psychological disposition and that, in its turn, has the capacity to affect what they do and how they do it. Peter Baelz says:

> We should think less of God's compelling the world to do what he wants and more of his persuading and enabling it of its own free will to do what he wants . . . At the human level it means that God acts through the re-direction of our thoughts and desires.[34]

This avoids any sense of divine manipulation of human agents to effect God's will in response to prayer, but some will see such psychological influence as no less a threat to human freedom. We have considered how our prayers for ourselves or others should meet with corresponding commitment on our part to act as best we can in support of such prayers. But that is not the same as God directly influencing human agents psychologically in order to stimulate action. We are still left feeling that our freedom has been attenuated somewhat by an influence which, however benign and divine, leaves us less in control of ourselves than genuine free will requires to be the case.

However, it is important to acknowledge ways in which prayer can impact for good on the thoughts and feelings of those who are the subjects of our prayers. The composer Gustav Mahler, as a child, would spend time praying for his sick mother and then ask her if she was better. 'No,' she would say, 'but I feel better.' She did not detect an improvement in

---

34. Baelz, *Does God Answer Prayer?* pp.34-35.

her physical condition, but knowing that her son prayed for her gave her comfort and enhanced her sense of well-being. That is why it is generally good to assure people of our prayers for them. Although any positive feelings this generates will surely be consistent with God's benign purposes, it is our care and concern for them, of which our prayers are an expression, that contributes to their feeling better and not any direct psychological intervention on God's part. We may still want to credit God with having ordered things in such a way that knowing themselves to be prayed for gives people a positive boost, but there is no sense in which free will has been compromised. Our decision to pray, and a person's knowledge of that decision, are what effect a beneficial change which will no doubt be in accordance with God's will, but will not be a result of direct divine intervention.

So it is that the tipping point has taken us into territory where we are focusing not so much on how little or how much God's sovereignty might be subject to self-limitation, but on the extent to which we must be prepared to bend our own freedom towards meeting the demands of our petitions and intercessions. And just as approaches located more towards the other end of the spectrum were subject to scrutiny on account of their threat to our freedom, so we have to ask whether we are now paying too high a price in terms of threats to God's sovereignty. Have we been so defensive of human freedom, and so indulgent towards modern world views, that God is reduced to the status of a concerned spectator who hears our prayers and takes them to heart, but does nothing to help unless it is in the form of us helping ourselves?

Vernon White has done more than enough to establish that special divine action in the world is a credible notion – indeed, a necessary one if God is to be God.[35] Here he is in the company of such giants of twentieth-century theology as Karl Barth and Helmut Thielicke, and even when such luminaries as Keith Ward, W. H. Vanstone and Peter Baelz come to more nuanced conclusions, still God's capacity to act creatively and providentially is not in dispute.[36]

The question then boils down to whether God does so act, particularly in response to our prayers, rather than whether he *can*, and if so, on what terms. The key to answering this question lies in how we understand God's relationship to the world he has made, and especially his relationship to his human creation. Consideration of this question takes us to the final stage along our sovereignty–free will spectrum.

6. Free will related

Philip Yancey is clear that 'prayer is a declaration of dependence on God'.[37] This statement is incontestable insofar as it sums up the relationship between a creature and his or her Creator. The Bible promotes the relationship between a potter and his clay to make the point (Romans 9:21), and because we believe God to be dependable when it comes to his love for us, this is a form of dependency we are happy to embrace. Yet it begs many questions about God's superiority and supremacy relative to our human nature. Does not such an asymmetrical relationship necessarily foster

35. White, *The Fall of a Sparrow*.
36. See especially W. H. Vanstone, *Love's Endeavour, Love's Expense* (DLT, 1977), and K. Ward, *God, Chance and Necessity* (Oxford, 1996).
37. Yancey, *Prayer: Does It Make Any Difference?*, p.27.

a culture of cowering fear, servility and resignation on the part of we who owe our very existence to an almighty God? Am I not a worm, and no man (Psalm 22:6), so that the best I can do is keep my head down, accommodate myself to the way things go in the world, and keep on as good terms as I can with my Lord and Master? Jonathan Aitken memorably described such a relationship with God as comparable to his relationship with his bank manager:

> I spoke to him politely, visited his premises intermittently, occasionally asked him for a small favour or overdraft to get myself out of difficulty, thanked him for his assistance, kept up the appearance of being one of his reasonably reliable customers, and maintained superficial contact with him on the grounds that one of these days he might come in useful.[38]

After his fall from grace, Aitken sought a more profound and mature relationship with God so that his prayer life became more mutual, intimate and personal.

The kind of relationship God seeks with us is not obsequious subservience on our part, nor effortless superiority on his. He does not want to dictate – he would rather delegate. He does not want to call the shots – he would rather wait upon our requests and respect our free will. He does not want to overrule our decisions or override our actions – he would rather come alongside us, to indwell and inspire us, so that our wills are aligned with his and our lives lived accordingly. For our part, such a relationship will require us to uphold the courtesies of praise, contrition and thanksgiving, but in

---

38. Jonathan Aitken, *Pride and Perjury* (Continuum, 2004), p.12.

such a way as to bring us closer to God rather than pushing us further apart. With Vincent Brümmer, we can confidently affirm that:

> All forms of prayer (including petition) affect the relation between God and man [sic], and therefore have a real effect on both . . . In petitionary prayer I do not renounce myself or my own desires . . . But I do renounce the use of constraint in getting God to grant my petition, and thereby I acknowledge both God's freedom as a person and my dependence on his free decision for granting whatever I ask of him. This petitionary attitude to God is a necessary condition for establishing a personal relation with God.[39]

This prompts the rather daring suggestion that prayer is more than a declaration of dependence: it is a declaration of interdependence, with both God and the petitioner affected by prayer, but not in such a way as to force the hand of either. It is no coincidence that this is analogous to the best kinds of human relationships whereby shared concerns and common causes are addressed without any sense of coercion or conflict of interest. It is often the case that when a couple are inclined to bicker or squabble over trivial things, they show a remarkable capacity to pull together in the face of really daunting challenges. At those times they know that whatever they face, they will face together, and so the relationship proves stronger than the odds stacked against them, and it is the relationship which will live on probably stronger now as a result of the trials it has endured.

---

39. Brümmer, *What Are We Doing When We Pray?*, pp.74, 78.

Perhaps we can best understand God's role in answer to our prayers along lines such as these. And, as Peter Baelz suggests, that may be enough. It certainly fits with much of what we have observed about God's doing and not doing which both science and ordinary experience raise and which disturb our faith.[40] It honours God's sovereignty because through our acts of adoration, confession and thanksgiving we know with whom we are in relationship. It also respects our freedom, as God's love puts his power at the service of our relationship with him and does not seek to overwhelm us.

The account of Jesus in the Garden of Gethsemane is most revelatory of his relationship with his father. He had no reservations about expressing his fears in relation to what confronted him, and his hopes for something different. Yet he knew that his father's love for him would not let him down, so he could pray, 'Not my will, but thine be done.' That relationship would survive the trial to come, and in the overall scheme of things it was the relationship that mattered most of all. What triumphed on the cross was the power of love – power in love with the world – and, like Jesus in Gethsemane, when we pray for ourselves and for others, it is the effect of our prayers on our relationship with God, with others and with the world he has made that matters most. We rejoice that God's relationship with us allows us, by his sovereign and loving will, to make our petitions and intercessions unto him; and we further rejoice that our relationship with God is such that in responding to our prayers God will do nothing to negate our freedom faithfully to face the future, whatever may befall.

---

40. See Baelz, *Does God Answer Prayer?*, p.50.

When Philip Yancey experiences what he calls 'the silence of God' in response to his prayers, he asks himself 'whether I have been primarily pursuing results from my prayer rather than companionship with God'.[41] In a similar vein, Helmut Thielicke asks whether we do not all too often set our hearts on the gift in the hand rather than on taking the hand of the giver. There are many people who will want to see impetratory prayer exclusively in terms of asking for things and looking to the sovereign power of God to deliver them. But for those at this end of our spectrum, it is taking the hand of the giver that seems to matter more than the gift itself.[42]

Prayer as a spectrum of possibilities

In order to summarise this spectrum of possibilities, we can take a situation which will quite typically be the subject of an intercessory prayer. John is a church member who has been recently admitted to hospital. Here are six sample intercessions to illustrate the various stages on our journey.

a. God, thou knowest – be it unto John according to thy word

Here we detect an emphasis on God's foreknowledge and predetermination when it comes to what happens for John. God's word in this case is essentially the Word which spoke creation into being, and within that Word is contained all that has been, is or will be. Willing God's will is indeed a form of prayer, but it leaves no room for God to act otherwise than already fore-ordained, and similarly there is no way we

---

41. Yancey, *Prayer: Does It Make Any Difference?*, p.195.
42. Helmut Thielicke, *How to Believe Again* (Collins, 1973), pp.90-100.

or anyone else can act for John in support of our prayer except insofar as God has factored our prayer and action into his predetermined providence. God's sovereignty is supreme and secure, but human free will and the kind of loving relationship between us and God which depends upon it, do not feature.

b. John is ill – let us remember him in a moment of silence

This is a form of prayer appropriate to Deism which flourished following the Enlightenment (see 'Sovereignty suspended' earlier in this chapter'). It argues that God has created the world to proceed without further activity on his part. He is like an absentee landlord who has designed, built, furnished and peopled the property and then suspended his sovereignty to leave it to run according to pre-set principles and without further involvement on his part. If this is so, then all we can do in prayer is remember John in his hour of need and leave it at that.

Such a prayer is not pointless. John may well be comforted by knowing we have thought about him in God's presence, and this act of remembrance may encourage us and others to undertake practical actions on his behalf. But God as sovereign Creator remains aloof, and our freedom is seriously constrained by the exigencies of a closed universe.

c. Please, God, heal John

This is predicated on God directly intervening in the world from time to time in miraculous ways. We have identified challenges to this view which are philosophical, moral and scientific as well as theological (see 'Sovereignty sometimes' earlier). But invoking God's sovereign power *in extremis* goes to the heart of what we assume the majority of people believe prayer to be about. To an extent this is true, but studies by Tania ap Siôn and Peter Collins of prayer requests left by visitors to an English Cathedral and a hospital chapel respectively, show that, while they may major on requests for healing, most do not address God at all.[43] This suggests an emerging disconnect between such requests and traditional understandings of intercessory prayer. Perhaps miracle as magic rather than miracle as divine providence is more to the fore here.

d. Please, God, work through us and the doctors to heal John

This contains no explicit reference to God intervening in a miraculous way. Here God's activity is limited to influencing or conscripting human agents to employ normal and natural procedures on John's behalf. As we have seen (see 'Free will conscripted' earlier in this chapter), this places a premium on the active engagement of people who pray with the object of their prayers. That is all to the good, but it also implies that God can be asked to use the agency of doctors, for example, to effect a positive outcome for John, and this distinct whiff of psychological or even physical manipulation does not sit well with advocates of free will. But there is potential in this scenario for God's sovereignty and our freedom to be kept in some form of dynamic equilibrium.

---

43. Giuseppe Giordan and Linda Woodhead (eds.), *A Sociology of Prayer* (Ashgate, 2015), pp.169-211.

e. Please, God, help John, his family and us to cope with his illness

Here God's activity is limited to influencing human attitudes and perspectives, but not physical nature. This avoids many of the pitfalls associated with an interventionist God, and praying for people to be strengthened to cope with a life crisis is consistent with what might be thought of as God's *métier*. After all, we gladly sing Harriet Auber's hymn:

> Our blest Redeemer, ere he breathed
> His tender last farewell,
> A guide, a Comforter, bequeathed
> With us to dwell.

But to what extent an indwelling amounts to an invasion is a moot point, and for some even this might be too much of a threat to our freedom. For others, this again seems to strike a balance between divine sovereignty and human free will, and is to be embraced accordingly.

f. God, we name John and his illness in your presence: thank you for inviting us to intercede for him, and so may our relationship to him and you be enriched

This very laboured petition seeks to capture the privilege of prayer as both evidence for and expression of our relationship with God who, though sovereign, wants us to freely intercede and inspires us to do so. There is little here for those looking for a miracle, but there is something profoundly affecting about such a relationship and the grace-filled love which God offers to us and hopes for in return. We have the freedom to accept or reject that love, and we have the freedom to accept or reject God's invitation to pray, so there is no threat to our free will in any of this. Furthermore, the quality of a relationship cannot be statistically measured in the way promoted by Francis Galton, so that prayer understood in this way does most to expose his category mistake. However, such a degree of divine condescension can seem close to abdication, and that can cause us to seriously question whether impetratory prayer as 'aiming at getting things by praying for them' is really in play at all.

Conclusion

The challenge before us is to judge the extent to which any points on our spectrum meet Vernon White's criteria quoted at the beginning of this chapter. Meeting the prerequisites of sovereignty, divine love, creaturely freedom and modern world views when trying to account for transcendent divine activity in the world is no easy task. This becomes all the more difficult when we factor in the emotional, relational and subjective dimensions pertaining to prayer in general, and impetratory prayer in particular.

It could well be that none of the approaches we have examined meets all the criteria all of the time, but all of them meet some of the criteria some of the time! That would be something to be expected, given that we are seeking to explicate in objective and conceptual terms an activity which taps into the metaphysical mysteries of a transcendent and ineffable deity – prayer is, indeed, a very peculiar practice. Where we find ourselves at any given moment on this spectrum of possibilities may well be determined by factors more psychological and circumstantial than strictly theological. That is fine insofar as our practice of prayer is always likely to range from urgently impulsive to deeply reflective on what we are really doing when we pray, whatever the circumstances and situations in which prayer plays a part, and we have sought to provide some analytical tools to aid such reflection.

Chapter four

Praying for all its worth

We have examined a number of ways in which prayer has been understood from a variety of perspectives, and we have done so with particular reference to petitionary and intercessory prayer. This range of possibilities has revealed philosophical and theological challenges which must be met if our petitions and intercessions are to stand up to scrutiny as more than just wishful thinking or even superstition.

It is fair to say that over the centuries impetratory prayer has proved to be more troublesome to philosophers than theologians. Especially since the dawn of the age of reason and science, the need to justify such a practice as logically coherent and empirically verifiable has dominated philosophical criticism and theological rejoinders. While for New Atheists such as Richard Dawkins and Christopher Hitchins this logical and scientific positivism has established the incoherence of prayer once and for all – and the burden of most Anglo-American analytical philosophy has been supportive of such scepticism – the emphasis in continental philosophy has been on the intelligibility and integrity of religious language with prayer treated as no less but, importantly, no more subject to suspicion and deconstruction than any other uses of language. This in its turn has resulted in post-modern philosophers being more open to the probity of impetratory prayer than in the less recent past. In this they have been supported by practitioners of sub-atomic physics who find sufficient provisionality and unpredictability amid the fundamental particles of matter to make divinely initiated occurrences in response to prayer at least hypothetically possible.

Meanwhile, theologians have had to contend with other kinds of challenges, notably the tension between God's sovereignty and our freedom – a tension which has dominated our discussion thus far. Belief in God as an omnipotent being who is able and willing to intervene in the world in miraculous ways was challenged not only by the assumptions of modern science, but also by the findings of psychology and psychiatry in what became known as the second Enlightenment. The psyche and subjectivity of individuals came to dominate accounts of what it means to be human, with free will and determinism hotly debated factors in human growth and development. To forfeit one's free will in acquiescence to external controls on belief and behaviour was condemned as 'bad faith', while respect for personal freedoms came to dominate the advocacy and protection of human rights. Anthropology has always been the handmaid of theology, but never more so than in the late twentieth century. All this in addition to the emergence of the so-called 'free will defence' in dealing with the problem of evil, and particularly acts of evil directly related to human agency.

So we have been living through an era when balancing human free will with belief in God's sovereignty has been a theological priority, and we have seen this reflected in much that has been said and written about prayer as petition and intercession. At places along our spectrum of possibilities we have suggested that this balance has been struck more effectively than elsewhere, but at no point can it be said that there is perfect equilibrium. Still, at all points we have identified positive themes which help towards a general appraisal of prayer as a good and proper practice for people of faith to pursue – and a perfectly plausible practice on the part of those whose faith is as yet tentative and unsure.

1. The answer is in the asking

We have already suggested that a prayer offered is a prayer received, and a prayer received is a prayer answered. But surely this requires some qualification. Can just any prayer be a prayer received? Is it not necessary for contrition and repentance to be in place before a prayer of confession can be received? Can a prayer of thanksgiving be received if the subject of that prayer is morally or spiritually unworthy? In such cases it is possible to argue that the prayer has not really been offered at all. It is a sham offering because it lacks sincerity and integrity.

However, in relation to petitionary and intercessory prayer, we might be wise to take more time to reflect before rushing to judgement about what is or is not an appropriate and acceptable offering. A prayer for what is logically impossible – e.g., that a triangle be the same shape as a square – cannot be considered appropriate. But beyond that, discrimination becomes rather difficult.

I recall sitting in a prayer group prior to an event as part of a parish mission, when I became aware of a colleague praying that the electrical socket in the meeting hall would be a 13 amp square pin. My immediate reaction was to bristle at the triviality and impertinence of such a prayer. 'Get up out of your chair,' I wanted to say, 'and go and see.'

Did he honestly believe that before uttering that petition the socket could be of one kind but would then mutate into something else? Could this prayer be considered a legitimate offering, and therefore be said to be received, let alone be answered?

Well, yes, because as I reflected on his earnest petition I realised that what was being articulated was an anxiety that things should go well and a fear that a technical hitch might prove troublesome. It was the anxiety and the fear which were being offered to God in prayer, and we can be confident that a God of love will not reject such an approach made in all good faith. As Karl Barth put it with characteristic directness:

> Man [sic] might ask God for anything. The whole of human egoism, the whole of human anxiety, cupidity, desire and passion, or at least the whole of human short-sightedness, unreasonableness and stupidity, might flow into prayer (and that by divine commandment!), as effluent from the chemical factories of Basel is discharged into the Rhine . . . But if God is not uneasy in this regard, we certainly need not be.[44]

For sure, as we have seen earlier and shall see again, a petition presented in such terms does require action on our part. My colleague did indeed go from the prayer meeting to check the socket, which turned out to be, in fact, a 13 amp square pin! Yet even if it had not been so, the speaking of the prayer with all its undertones of anxiety and fear is on all

---

44. Karl Barth, *Church Dogmatics III 4* (T. & T. Clark, 1960), p.100.

fours with the prayers offered in relation to circumstances and situations which cause us concern and about which we articulate specific hopes, but about which we do not know what is actually the case. When we offer intercessions for someone undergoing an operation or attending an important interview, we will not know how things are going in exact detail, but our prayers express our concern for those involved, and we can be sure that what is of concern to us will be of concern to God, and our prayers will be received accordingly.

It is difficult to believe that God can possibly care about the details of my day-to-day life, and many believe he doesn't. But he does care about the fact that those things concern me, and concern me enough to take them to the Lord in prayer. This means that little or nothing can be ruled out of bounds when it comes to what we can appropriately bring to God in our intercessions for others and in petitions for ourselves. Many saintly Christians have been unsure about the propriety of praying for themselves. The mystic Meister Eckhart refused to 'pray the rich and loving God for such trifles' as to help him recover from an illness.[45] But in the Lord's Prayer, 'daily bread' effectively stands for our everyday needs, including all those things which constitute our well-being. To be concerned about such things, especially when we fear for their loss or hope for their improvement, is perfectly natural, and God wants to hear about them.

The belief that God does indeed want to hear from us when it comes to what concerns and dis-eases us goes to the heart of what impetratory prayer is all about. It is not simply

---

45. Yancey, *Prayer: Does It Make Any Difference?*, p.310.

a case of us having a kind of therapeutic need to unburden ourselves to our creator. God, as creator, especially desires to hear from us because that is how loving relationships work most effectively. Keith Ward reminds us that God always has several options open to him with respect to his providential activity, but it will always be better for God to act in response to a request rather than choose an option unilaterally.[46] Can we be confident that a prayer offered is a prayer received? Yes, because God in his love and wisdom wills to receive the prayers we offer – and God's will can be trusted.

But is a prayer received indeed a prayer answered? This question becomes all the more urgent in the light of our readiness to include as wide a range of prayers as possible in what God deems to be acceptable. Notwithstanding the fact that many prayers are offered for things which revelation, reason and intuition suggest might be inappropriate, and that we are challenged to acquaint ourselves as best we can with what God has revealed to us of his acceptable will, still behind even such apparently inappropriate prayers there is a human being hoping to be heard and in need of grace.

The Prodigal Son practised a petition he would make to his father once he resolved to return home from the far country. But before he could get it all said, the father came to meet him, embraced him and restored him to his place. In a sense, the appropriateness or otherwise of the petition mattered less than the hurt and heartfelt hopes that lay within it. For that boy, a prayer received was a prayer answered, and we have every reason to believe that this will likewise be so for us and for others. We rest our petitions and intercessions with God

---

46. Keith Ward, *Divine Action* (Collins, 1990), chapter 9.

whose loving purposes must ultimately prevail, and when we know our prayers to be received by such a one, then we know they have been answered in whatever may happen thereafter. The American gospel singer Leo Welch wrote a song entitled 'You can't hurry God', which included the line:

He may not come when you want him,
But he's always right on time.[47]

Which brings us to our second key theme.

2. The answer is in what happens

Jean Pierre de Caussade (1675–1751) spoke of 'the sacrament of the present moment'. To pray is to acknowledge God's involvement in everything and every moment so that what happens is where God is to be found, and is the answer to our prayer if only we will attend to it.[48]

This is a difficult line to follow when we pray for something which we have good scriptural and doctrinal reasons for believing is consistent with the character and purposes of God, but which results in a very different outcome. All the signs are that our prayer has been ignored or, even worse, treated with cruel cynicism. This is the issue Jesus tackled head on when he referred to human fathers not giving their children stones when they ask for bread, or a snake when they ask for a fish. He goes on: 'If you, then, who are evil, know how to give good gifts to your children, how much more will your Father in heaven give good things to those who ask him!' (Matthew 7:9-11).

---

47. Leo Welch, 'You can't hurry God', from the album *Sabougla Voices* (2014).
48. See Jean Pierre de Caussade, *Self-abandonment to Divine Providence* (Collins, 1971).

The clear message is that God does not do cynicism. What results from our prayers will not amount to ridiculing what we have asked for ourselves or others. But does that entitle Jesus to conclude that God gives 'good things to those who ask him'? From our point of view, what happens following our prayers often feels far from good, and we are left wondering why.

We might simply accept that God knows best when it comes to what is good in any given situation, and he does us a favour when he declines to go along with our petitions. Shakespeare's Menacrates captures this sentiment when he declares:

> We, ignorant of ourselves,
> beg often our own harms, which the wise powers
> deny us for our good; so find we profit
> by losing our prayers.[49]

So the mother who prayed that her son would come to visit her by sailing on the Titanic will give thanks when she learns that he missed the boat. God as sovereign must be credited with knowledge above and beyond that to which we can aspire, so that we can readily accept and give thanks for his overriding of our prayers in such a situation. The outcome for our prayers has been good, notwithstanding that it has been other than that for which we prayed.

However, we struggle to reconcile ourselves to such a vindication of God's superior knowledge when, for example, our prayer is for a hostage to be released unharmed and he is in fact executed. While we can attribute that to the abuse

---

49. William Shakespeare, *Anthony and Cleopatra*, Act 2, Scene 1.

of God's gift of free will on the part of the hostage takers, we cannot say as much when we pray for the safe return home of a fishing boat and it sinks in a freak storm at sea. This severely challenges any resolve we have to keep faith with God's superior wisdom, let alone Jesus' assurance that God will not respond to our prayers in ways that amount to us being tricked or mistreated. This is the point at which the poet William Cowper pressed the 'mystery' button:

> God moves in a mysterious way
> his wonders to perform;
> he plants his footsteps in the sea,
> and rides upon the storm.[50]

God's purposes are pursued as much in the violent storm as in the calm which follows it, even if they lie too deep for our understanding. Blaise Pascal agonised over this issue:

> I know not which is most profitable to me, health or sickness, wealth or poverty, nor anything else in the world. That discernment is hidden among the secrets of your Providence, which I adore, but do not seek to fathom.[51]

Cowper puts it this way:

> Deep in unfathomable mines
> of never-failing skill
> he treasures up his bright designs,
> and works his sovereign will.[52]

---

50. William Cowper (1731–1800), 'God moves in a mysterious way'.
51. Quoted in William James, *The Varieties of Religious Experience* (The Modern Library, 1936), p.281.
52. Cowper, 'God moves in a mysterious way'.

That being the case, we must be courageous in the face of danger, just as Jesus challenged his disciples to have faith even as the storm was raging in Matthew's version of the stilling of the storm (Matthew 8:23-27 [53]):

> Ye fearful saints, fresh courage take;
> the clouds ye so much dread
> are big with mercy, and shall break
> in blessings on your head.[54]

It may be hard for us to see what is good about a violent storm, especially when it puts at risk the life of someone for whom we have prayed to come home safely. But when we concede the frailty of our understanding, and the invincibility of God's love, then we have grounds to be confident that all will be well:

> Judge not the Lord by feeble sense,
> but trust him for his grace;
> behind a frowning providence
> he hides a smiling face.[55]

And this is not some kind of knowing smile or even a smirk – the sort of thing implied by the well-known saw: 'If you want to make God smile, tell him your plans!' No, this is the smiling face of one who has the whole world in his hands and wills for his world only sweetness and light:

> His purposes will ripen fast,
> unfolding every hour;
> the bud may have a bitter taste,
> but sweet will be the flower.[56]

---

53. See John Saxbee, *WayMARKers* (Kevin Mayhew, 2013), p.22.
54, 55, 56. Cowper, 'God moves in a mysterious way'.

Cowper concludes that:

> Blind unbelief is sure to err,
> and scan his work in vain;
> God is his own interpreter,
> and he will make it plain.[57]

Just as 'love has its reasons which reason knows not',[58] so God has his reasons for all that happens, not least all that happens in response to our prayers, and his interpretation of events which we find distressing and inexplicable will eventually be made clear. There is a sense, a good and benign sense, in the outworking of God's providence, and even if we must endure the bitter taste of a prayer apparently nipped in the bud, we can have faith that the flower which eventually blossoms will be a thing of grace and beauty.

It was just such an account of God's providence which so disturbed Ivan Karamazov in Dostoevsky's *The Brothers Karamazov*.[59] He concluded that there could never be an outcome which might justify the hounding to death of a small child. He would respectfully 'return his ticket' and abandon his faith in God. This must be an option for Ivan and others who choose to exercise their free will by respectfully returning the ticket. It goes to the heart of that wrestling with God which punctuates the scriptures from Genesis to Gethsemane.

We cannot escape such agonising over the horrors which confront us directly or indirectly, and the ubiquitous nature of mass media results in us being observers of such horrors on a daily basis. The Book of Psalms provides us with more

---

57. Cowper, 'God moves in a mysterious way'.
58. Blaise Pascal, *Pensées*, iv. 277.
59. Moscow, 1880.

than enough examples of how to weep and gnash our teeth as lamentation follows lamentation. We may sometimes take comfort from the scriptural permission this gives us to wrestle with God and even vent our anger towards him. We may be humbled by the way in which Job and Jesus never lost faith in God's purposes. But we may also find ourselves pursued by doubt and despair to the point where we resolve to return the ticket.

But it is not the only option. We can choose not to go down the route of despair and meaninglessness in the face of such unmitigated evil. Rather, we can believe in God's 'mysterious way' and pray with the assurance of those who know that their prayers will be heard, received and answered – and take comfort in the knowledge that what happens is the answer from the perspective of eternity.

St Augustine wrestled long and hard with these issues and recorded in his *Confessions*:

> You, who are truth, reside everywhere to answer all who ask counsel of you, and in one act reply to all, though all seek counsel on different matters. And you answer clearly, but all do not hear clearly. All ask what they wish, but do not always hear the answer they wish. That man is your best servant who is not so much concerned to hear from you what he wills as to will what he hears from you.

On this account there is no such things as unanswered prayer – 'what happens' is the answer even when 'what happens' is other than we asked.

We can certainly say that this approach to impetratory prayer strikes an appropriate balance between honouring God's sovereignty and respect for our free will. God's loving purposes ultimately prevail, but not because the course of this world has been predetermined, nor because physical events, human actions or psychological responses have been divinely manipulated. As events in the world evolve through natural processes and humanity's freely chosen decisions and actions, so God's sovereign will at work in and through those events ensures that nothing counts for nothing and that everything, including our prayers, works together for good. The exercise of our freedom in our thinking, speaking, acting and praying plays a part in shaping the kind of future through which God's good purposes are realised, so that we are not just providing threads for the master to weave into a perfect pattern, but actually helping to give that pattern its final form. To see what happens as a result of our prayers as contributing to the shaping of a future consistent with God's sovereignty and our freedom is to see whatever happens as the answer to our prayers and the florescence of faith – and 'sweet will be the flower'.

David Wilkinson repeatedly refers to 'unanswered prayer' when what is really at issue is prayer answered otherwise than as requested.[60] Following Jesus' example, he draws extensively on the relationship between parent and child as analogous to our relationship with God. Surely, key to such a relationship is that a child's request will not be ignored or belittled. It will be given the parent's full attention so that what happens will define the response. It can never be said of a good and

---

60. Wilkinson, *When I Pray, What Does God Do?*, p.216.

loving parent that their child's request has been ignored – answered otherwise than as specifically requested, perhaps, but not ignored. Neither can it be said of God that a petition or intercession has gone unanswered in the sense of being ignored. And if it does not go unanswered, then it is answered in terms of what happens then and thereafter. If, as Wilkinson says, 'the key to prayer is how we understand God',[61] then a parental model entails that God always answers prayer, so that what happens is received as response rather than rejection.

Wilkinson reflects on his own experience of 'unanswered prayer'. He concedes:

> that the most transforming moments have been as I have lamented and even expressed anger towards God in worship. Indeed, they have been a kind of cathartic experience which in its own mysterious way becomes an unexpected positive outcome to prayer.[62]

Surely this equates to a prayer received – and answered.

There are resonances here with biblical injunctions to be thankful (see Ephesians 5:4; 1 Thessalonians 5:18). The Book of Common Prayer avers in the Order for Holy Communion that: 'It is very meet, right, and our bounden duty, that we should at all times, and in all places, give thanks unto thee, O Lord, Holy Father, Almighty, Everlasting God.' This sounds counter-intuitive, given that we are generally conditioned to limit thankfulness to those things we consider to be good, fortunate and welcome. Giving thanks 'at all times and in all places' implies an attitude of mind and soul which is disposed towards gratitude even when there seems to be little that is positive to be said about the situation in which we and/or others find ourselves.

61. Wilkinson, *When I Pray, What Does God Do?*, p.183.
62. Wilkinson, *When I Pray, What Does God Do?*, pp.108-9.

Such an attitude was evident in the life of the German pastor Martin Rinkart, who during the ravages of the Thirty Years' War was burying up to 50 people a week in his parish and yet could still find it within himself to write the hymn 'Now thank we all our God'.

This peculiarly religious take on thankfulness has been explored by Paul L. Holmer. He sees the capacity to be thankful 'at all times and in all places' as a gift of grace. It liberates us from a narrowly conditional understanding of gratitude as limited to a culturally agreed range of benefits. Because our sense of values and virtues transcends such limited grounds for gratitude, and because our perspective is that of eternity not time, we adopt thankfulness as a permanent state of mind even, or perhaps especially, when worldly considerations would counsel otherwise. Holmer concludes:

> Instead of being stripped of feelings and pathos, as we often are in the tragic everyday world, we are being offered also new joys, a peace that the world does not provide, and a thankfulness that can survive anything that happens.[63]

It is this conversion to a whole new perspective on thankfulness that also informs our belief that the answer to prayer is what happens, because now 'what happens' is perceived and received not as mere fate, to the inevitability of which we must resign ourselves, but as an outcome filtered through our faith in God who receives our prayers and, through what happens, answers them in the context and currency of eternity.

---

63. Paul L. Holmer, *Thinking the Faith with Passion* (Cambridge: James Clarke, 2013), pp.326-327.

However, we must now take account of the responsibilities which we are required to honour as a result of our being able to be partners with God in his providential activity through the offering of our petitions and intercessions.

3. The answer is in the doing

It is likely that, apart from in relation to prayer, for most of us the word 'petition' relates to a collection of signatures in support of a particular cause. If you sign a petition against, for example, throwing litter in a public place but habitually leave your paper cup lying around for others to pick up, you will probably be condemned as a hypocrite, and rightly so. As the saying goes, if you are not part of the solution, then you are part of the problem.

And so it is with petitionary prayers. That is why Ian Ramsey and others make so much of practical action as integral to such prayers if they are to be truly authentic and acceptable. To pray about something and then fail to act in support of that prayer when you have the ability and opportunity to do so is tantamount to hypocrisy. When we pray, we may already have in mind the ways in which we will apply ourselves to the matter in hand, or it may be the very offering of the prayer that prompts us individually or communally to get stuck in. Either way, we do what we can to avoid charges of hypocrisy or projecting on to God responsibilities for action which, at least in part, rest with us. To that extent, answers to prayer are to be found in the responsive and responsible actions of those who pray.

However, all that said, it is worth reminding ourselves of Duc de la Rochefoucauld's maxim: 'Hypocrisy is homage paid by vice to virtue.'[64] In other words, we may by our action or inaction know ourselves to be hypocritical, and that knowledge, with the unease it causes us, forces upon us some recognition as to where virtue lies. One rarely acknowledged dimension of impetratory prayer is that it challenges us at least to try to articulate concerns and requests for ourselves, for other people and for the world around us which are righteous in the sight of God, and therefore virtuous in their content and intention. If we do fail to follow through with appropriate action in support of such prayers, still the very uttering of them has a positive part to play in our moral and spiritual formation – and due homage will have been paid by vice to virtue.

4. Prayer as self-giving

In his original and stimulating book *The Widening Circle*, Graham Tomlin effectively argues that priesthood is far too important to be left to 'Priests'.[65] Priests in the form of ordained ministers have a vital role to play in the economy of salvation, but it is not exercised apart from the rest of the Church. Rather, the role of such priests is to enable all members of the Body of Christ to become a kingdom of priests interceding prayerfully and practically in Christ's name on behalf of the human race which, in its turn, has been chosen to exercise a priestly role between God and creation. This means that such sacrificial overtones as apply to the exercise of priesthood apply to all humanity on behalf of creation, and to all believers on behalf of humanity. At the heart of Christ's High

---

64. Duc de la Rochefoucauld, *Maximes*, 218.
65. Graham Tomlin, *The Widening Circle* (SPCK, 2014).

Priesthood is his self-sacrificial intercession for the world, and it is in 'joining in' with his mediatorial mission that we and all people fulfil our divine calling. This purposefully locates our petitions and intercessions with the widening circle of priestly vocation and, as importantly, within the self-sacrificial work of Christ.

This is a vital insight, because it provides a counter to the misbegotten notion that the kind of prayer we have been considering has about it the whiff of narrow self-interest. This can be so even when we intercede for others, because we can be accused of favouring those nearest and dearest to us, praying in such generalised terms that we succumb to blandness or irresponsibly shifting on to God matters which we should be tackling ourselves.

While, as we have seen, there can be substance to such criticisms and we have to address them, what they fail to acknowledge is that far from being selfish or self-serving, impetratory prayer is costly and self-giving. Certainly, intercessory prayer is good for us. It can develop our sensitivity and compassion so helping us to become better people. It can give us a sense of purposeful involvement in the situations which prompt our prayers. And, yes, it can give us a warm glow of self-satisfaction as a by-product of our concern for others. These benefits to ourselves must not be the sole or primary motive for our prayers, but they can be accepted as blessings upon us even as we give of ourselves sacrificially in interceding for others.

Such prayer is self-giving because it entails a challenge to us to actively give of ourselves in support of our prayers. It is self-giving because it requires us to immerse ourselves in God's word and will for the world so that we can pray with wisdom and discernment. But above all, it is self-giving because, in the words of Michael Ramsey, it commits us 'to be with someone [God] on behalf of others', so that time with God cannot be solely for our own sake. Prayers for our own needs and desires are no less acceptable than prayers for others, but are only acceptable when prayers for others are offered as well.[66]

The self-sacrificial nature of intercessory prayer is most powerfully exemplified by those individuals and communities who deliberately keep their own needs simple so that intercession for others can be always to the fore. Members of certain religious communities are clearly so disposed as are, for example, members of the Mothers' Union who can no longer attend meetings but commit to praying at home for the work of the MU around the world. Prayer positions us between God and God's world to make our petitions and supplications through Jesus Christ who, as our great High Priest, ever intercedes for us, his priestly people.

5. Prayer as solidarity

One of the best attested effects of intercessory prayer is the reassurance and encouragement it gives to those for whom prayers are offered. This will certainly be so when people are aware of such prayers for them, but there is ample testimony to the effect that people *in extremis* are acutely aware of bring prayed for even when they have no idea by whom, when or where. There is a sort of telepathic feel to this sense of not being alone or forgotten.

---

66. Michael Ramsey, *Canterbury Pilgrim* (London, 1974), p.60.

A friend of mine prayed regularly for an east European pastor held in solitary confinement for several years. From time to time his guards would taunt him to the effect that no one cared for him. 'Ah, but there is someone who cares,' he replied, 'because I feel his prayers for me.'

In 1915, as the First World War intensified, a young Welshman called Herbert Richards described the awfulness of trench life:

> I was staying last week about half a mile from the fireline. It was allfull [*sic*] on times there with the rolling of the guns. You could think that the end of the world had come. The German coalboxes were droping [*sic*] quite near to us rocking the houses down and shaking the place but I am still alive. It's the One Above I am to thank for all this. I believe that you are all praying for me.[67]

Perhaps we can use by way of an analogy the provision of air cover for an army battling away on the ground. Knowing that such air cover is there can make all the difference to the morale of those who might otherwise feel they are fighting a lonely war. Can we think of intercessory prayer for someone fighting against serious illness as a kind of air cover for them? It certainly seems to explain that sense of solidarity experienced by people in such situations, and must be seen as one of the greatest blessings bestowed through prayer.

We may not always know the exact details of someone's situation – in fact, we may not know them personally at all. But simply naming them as we come before God in prayer

---

67. National Library of Wales. E. K. Jones papers, 19 March 1915.

carries the gift of our concern and goodwill, and that may be enough to reassure them, through the mysterious workings of God's grace, that above them hovers a canopy of care.

After the Second World War, Britain was in the grip of extreme austerity as the government sought to foster recovery. The Americans were generally less afflicted on the domestic front and it was usual for US citizens to post what became known as Care Parcels to friends and relatives in the UK. After a while, parcels began to arrive addressed to 'someone hungry somewhere in England'. A practice hitherto restricted to known and identified people in need was extended to take in people not known personally to the donors but still able to benefit from their thoughtfulness and generosity. So it is with prayers offered thoughtfully and generously for the relief and well-being of people who, although not known personally to the intercessor, can nonetheless benefit from those prayers by God's grace. That is what we are about when we pray in general for people and situations beyond our immediate ken but nevertheless with a claim on our sympathy and solidarity.

Likewise, during dark days in South America when dissidents were being 'disappeared' by a military dictatorship on a regular basis, an Easter Service was held at which the names of the 'disappeared' were read out, and after each name a voice from the congregation would shout 'presente'. Through prayer, the disappeared reappeared through the assertion of solidarity at the heart of the Easter liturgy. Whatever our petitions and intercessions may or may not achieve in terms of the direct granting of specific requests, if we can be confident that those for whom we pray experience that canopy of care and the assurance of our solidarity, then there is much for which we and they can be thankful.

Here, mention should be made of solidarity generated by prayer offered by groups, communities or even nations on a coordinated basis. For many critics, the idea of people being exhorted to participate in Days of Prayer for rain or peace or some other purpose is risible. They mock the notion that the more people there are praying for a particular outcome, the more likely that outcome will come to pass. Like signatures on a petition or protesters on a march, the more there are, the more likely it is that councillors or politicians will grant what is wanted. Likewise, God is presumed to be susceptible to numerical strength when deciding how to respond to prayer.

Of course, this entirely misses the point of such calls for mass pray-ins, even if the way these things are sometimes promoted seems to collude with the 'those who shout loudest, longest and in greatest number are most likely to be heard' school of prayer. But in reality, the chief purpose of such days or waves of prayer is to express solidarity with a particular cause, to raise consciousness as to the issues at stake and to promote appropriate action to deliver what is desired.

It is easy to be cynical about calls to prayer which seem to cancel each other out, such as populations on either side in a war praying for victory. But behind it all is a passion to secure the protection, welfare and prosperity of a community, and to see right prevail even if delivery of those outcomes across the board is impossible and/or interpretations of what is right are incompatible. Surely it is this passion, however diversely expressed, which touches the heart of a God of love and, receiving it as such, God responds accordingly.

6. Prayer and blessing

Tomlin asserts, 'The Church's priestly calling is to bless the world in Christ . . . not just to pronounce blessing, but to be a blessing.' He goes on to expand this point in terms of the Church being a blessing 'by its very presence in the world . . . a visible reminder of the on-going commitment of God to his Creation'. It is 'a means of channelling God's blessing to humanity [by] being a community that shows another way of life, another pattern of social relating than the one we are used to in regular human societies'. By no means least, 'the Church also seeks to be a blessing through acts of goodness'.[68] He does not refer specifically to prayer as a means whereby the Church is a blessing to the world, but he would surely agree that intercession is right up there with social action when it comes to 'acts of goodness'.

When I became vicar of a parish in Plymouth, I dutifully began each day by walking the couple of hundred yards from the vicarage to the church, opening the door, tolling the bell and saying Morning Prayer. No one joined me, and when I caught a very bad cold I decided that sitting in a cold church first thing in the morning was not necessary, and I took to staying at home to say my prayers. Then gradually, often in light-hearted conversations in the street or in the pub, I was made aware that people missed the ringing of the bell. They joked about it in terms of knowing it was time to get up, or that they were late for the bus, because they heard the bell. But behind all that, I detected a sense that they consciously or subconsciously valued the fact that someone was praying for them and their community even if they found prayer

68. Tomlin, *The Widening Circle*, p.104.

difficult themselves. The bell and the prayer it signified was experienced as a blessing.

Later, when I moved to Lincoln, I was made aware of how my great predecessor, Bishop Edward King, let it be known that he stood at the window of his palace high on the hill early each morning and prayed for the workers as they made their way to the factories below – and they felt blessed. When he died, they lined the route for his funeral.

We also need to take note of so-called 'vicarious faith', as people project on to churchgoers their often inchoate but nonetheless sincere religious sentiment.[69] This sentiment comes to the fore when a tragedy of some kind occurs in a local community. It is likely that the news report of the event will include a reference to prayers being said in the parish church, together with an interview with the vicar to confirm that this is the case. A praying church clearly makes an important contribution to how people cope with such situations. This adds to a sense that petitionary and intercessory prayer, for all its philosophical and theological complexities, serves as a simple but profound blessing in a society which may be far less secular than many sociologists are inclined to suggest.

The French sociologist Marcel Mauss has done more than most to reflect on prayer as a social phenomenon. He concentrates mainly on the relationship between prayer as an individual practice and prayer as a group experience. He does not seem to have much to say about how the prayers of an individual or a small group can be owned and embraced by the wider community as *their* prayers offered,

---

69. See W. Carr (ed.), *Say One for Me* (SPCK, 1992) and J. Saxbee, *No Faith in Religion* (O Books, 2009).

not just for them but on their behalf and in their name. He defines prayers as 'oral, religious rites that aim at modifying something profane by conferring a sacred characteristic upon it'.[70] To such a definition, 'vicarious' prayer adds another dimension insofar as communities experiencing a collective sense of shock, gratitude, sorrow or celebration look to those who pray to confer a 'sacred characteristic' on those experiences. This is a through and through priestly ministry in the sense advocated by Tomlin, and confers not only a 'sacred characteristic' but also a redemptive blessing.

We need to note that early Christian liturgies included petitions and intercessions in the Eucharistic Prayer, and some still do. This is entirely appropriate because it directly associates such prayer with the offering being made at the altar and also confirms that when we pray we do so in obedience to Christ's command and in remembrance of him. Whenever we pray, we are caught up in our Lord's heavenly intercession, and never more so than when we celebrate the Lord's Supper and rehearse the Canon of the Mass.

7. Prayer and waiting upon God

Impetratory prayer can feel like a tug of war between what we want and what God wills – between our freedom to choose and God's right to rule. This is the sovereignty–free will tension to which we have alluded so often. We have traced this tension along a spectrum, and at each stage we have shown impetratory prayer to be both illuminated and

---

70. M. Mauss, *Oeuvres 1969–74*, Vol. I, pp. 413-4. See also Giordan and Woodhead, *A Sociology of Prayer*, p.11.

challenged. We have noted that some points on the spectrum seem better than others when it comes to balancing these two imperatives. Now we might reflect on a dynamic within this process which gives to our petitions and intercessions some added value.

By and large, we are inclined to be impatient with impediments to the exercise of our freedom. This is particularly so when we are physically restrained or find ourselves prevented by rules and regulations from doing what we want to do. Being at liberty to be ourselves and express ourselves without undue constraints on our liberty matters to us, and one of those constraints we find most frustrating is to be kept waiting for what we want. Whatever might be said about the merits of anticipation and the virtue of patience, taking the waiting out of wanting has become something of a modern-day mantra. In affluent societies where daily need for food, shelter, warmth, etc. is routinely met with money to spare, there is the ability to acquire possessions and access experiences by right as customers and consumers. What we do not need, we may still want – and we want it now!

One thing prayer does for us is curb our impatience when it comes to having all our desires not only known, but met as of right. That is why waiting upon God in prayer is such an important discipline. In a sense it can be said that instead of taking the waiting out of wanting, prayer takes the wanting out of waiting. This means that simply by coming before God reflectively and thoughtfully we put our wants, be they for ourselves or others, into perspective. We may even come to find that in the light of God's will revealed in and through our prayers, what we want is not what we thought we wanted at all. Or, at least, we come to see what we wanted in a new light and amend our priorities accordingly.

God wants us to make our requests known to him because that is central to a mature and reciprocal relationship. But he also wants us to make such requests known because in the very act of doing so we take time to reflect on that for which we ask, and wait upon God who loves his free but often foolish creatures, and wills for them to want what he knows to be wise.

8. Prayer and our relationship with God

In the 1980s, attention focused on an essay by Eleanor Stump entitled 'Petitionary Prayer'.[71] She explored the philosophical problems encountered when petitions are made to a God who is believed to be both all powerful and all good. They are the problems to which we have already drawn attention, and her conclusion is the one towards which we have been tending.

While God's power and sovereignty can be secured by postulating total predetermination and/or occasional interventions of a miraculous kind, we are left to wonder how anything other than a totally autocratic and manipulative relationship between the Creator and his creatures could be possible. Such a relationship leaves little room for the creatures to respond to their creator with love – or hate. Only when such responses are made freely and voluntarily can that be so, and God's desire for a loving relationship is manifest in his gift to us of free will. God's power resides in the granting

---

71. Eleanor Stump, 'Petitionary Prayer' in J. Huston (ed.), *Is it Reasonable to Believe in God?*, (Handsel, 1984), pp.131-151.

of a gift, and God's love resides in his granting this particular gift. It is in many respects a risky and, as the cross of Christ testifies, a costly gift, but it is one which ensures that it is God's love in relationship which takes precedence over God's absolutely sovereign but solitary power.

This leads Stump to conclude that petitionary prayer is a function of the developing relationship between God and humanity: asking makes a difference not to God only or to the asker only, but also to the relationship between them. This is confirmed by Vincent Brümmer: 'All forms of prayer (including petition) affect the *relation* between God and the person who prays and therefore have a *real* effect on both.'[72]

The dramatic implications of this conclusion become clear when we compare it to how prayer was commonly understood in the Graeco-Roman world. Cicero wrote, 'We do not pray to Jupiter to make us good, but to give us material benefits.'[73] This reduces impetratory prayer to the interaction between a supplicant and his supplier. We take delivery of what has been ordered and so the deal is done. The relationship, such as it is, has little or no qualitative characteristics. Indeed, the more impersonal and business-like it is, the better for all concerned.

Christians, on the other hand, do not see themselves as doing business with God on such a basis. It is the God who brought his people out of captivity in Egypt, who chastened them through the Prophets, restored them after Exile and redeemed them through Christ to whom they pray. Having

---

72. Brümmer, *What Are We Doing When We Pray?*, p.39 (his emphasis).
73. Quoted in Yancey, *Prayer: Does It Make Any Difference?*, p.143

been through so much together, there must be more to the relationship than the mere placing of an order for 'material benefits'. Praise, penitence and thanksgiving all play their part in forming a relationship conditioned by love and within which petitions and intercessions are offered as tokens of love and answered in the name of love. Contrary to Cicero's contention, prayer is not only about getting a god to do something. It is also about helping us to be something we might not otherwise be, except that God invites us to take his hand and so receive as from his hand the response to our prayers. That way goodness lies – God's goodness in receiving our prayers, and our good nurtured through the way this prayerful relationship with God teaches and trains us in ways of righteousness.

How different all this is from Homer's goddesses of prayer, as:

They limp and halt,
they're all wrinkled, drawn, they squint to the side,
can't look you in the eye, and always bent on duty,
trudging after Ruin, maddening, blinding Ruin.
But Ruin is strong and swift – She outstrips them all,
loping a march, skipping across the whole wide earth
to bring mankind to grief.
And the prayers trail after, trying to heal the wounds.[74]

When Jesus' disciples asked him to teach them to pray, they did so within a pagan culture where prayer was characterised by Cicero's cynicism and Homer's nihilism. How comforted

---

74. Homer, *Iliad* 9, 502-6.

they must have been when he enjoined them to approach the God of Creation as 'Our Father' – and so are we.

Or so we should be, because it is all too easy to take for granted this quality of relationship with God. Just as we can devalue the significance of the Eucharist by 'tripping lightly to the altar', so we can belittle the preciousness and privilege of prayer by turning the considered sharing of our hopes and fears with God our loving Father into a catalogue of procurement from the all-powerful provider. And that brings us to a point which undergirds our sense that petitionary and intercessory prayer is essentially relational and reciprocal. Throughout all our considerations there has been a misunderstanding that needs to be rectified and a principle that needs to be reaffirmed.

Clearly Cicero was not alone in thinking that prayer was merely a matter of asking for things. Neither was he wrong insofar as the very definition of impetratory prayer entails aiming at getting things by praying for them. However, he was wrong in his assumption that prayer is a kind of mechanism for tapping into the power possessed by the gods to dispense benefits, and at least sometimes to do so on request. We make a major mistake if we follow him in thinking of prayer in those terms. The God of the philosophers is more than anything a divinity in possession of limitless power because that is what is assumed to define deity, with little else needing to be said. He is a God who speaks through earthquake, wind and fire, and these are 'acts of God' because only God has the power to create and control them. For theologians, on the other hand, there is the 'still, small voice of calm' which God speaks through the elements, and so power is tempered by love.

When we make our petitions and intercessions, are we simply appealing to a source of power to supply what is wanted? Often it seems as though we are, especially when we pray out of sheer desperation. Such ejaculatory prayers are not illegitimate, for surely God knows and understands the circumstances in which they arise. But they are far from being the core currency in the economy of prayer. When we make our supplications unto God on a regular, thoughtful and considered basis, then we are most likely to look beyond God's power and see that for which we ask and our privilege in asking as links in a relationship of love. Then we make every effort to frame our prayers in ways consistent with what we believe to be God's loving purposes for the world, and we receive what happens consequent to our prayers as gifts of love. Much confusion around so-called unanswered prayer arises from the feeling that power has failed to deliver in response to our requests when, in fact, it is power as love which responds – power in love with the world.

To write these words is far easier than speaking them, especially when relating to situations of great distress, and to people who are too battered and torn to see through their tears a God of love who disposes his power for their good when he seems only to have turned their prayers against them. Yet on our belief in the ultimate invincibility of God's love for the world we rest our faith, because he loved the world so much as to give his only Son, that those who believe in him should not perish, but have everlasting life (John 3:16).

God does not play fast and loose with our freedom, nor does he gratuitously use his power to destabilise the way things go in the world. The only conditions he imposes on the exercise of his power are those which facilitate a loving relationship with his creation, and the self-limitation on his power is always so that this relationship of love can flourish. Our calling as Christians in relation to those who face bewilderment or even anger in the face of apparently unanswered prayer, ourselves included, is not to seek to defend God's use or non-use of power, but to profess God's love as the power in our lives which matters most, and to show and share *that* love, in word and deed, as best we can. To put power to the service of love seems counter-intuitive at a time when power is seen as the lever of choice when it comes to effecting change. But it is love which gives prayer its power – power in love with the world.

Philip Kerr's novel *Prayer*[75] features Special Agent Gil Martins, whose once strong religious faith has been destroyed by the gratuitous violence he deals with day by day. He is asked to investigate a series of unexplained deaths of victims known for their liberal views. When a woman tells Gil that these men have been killed by prayer, he questions her sanity. Yet as the evidence mounts, he begins to wonder if there might be something in what she says. The assumption Kerr relies upon is that most people today would think her mad because only a deranged person would believe that prayer can be directly instrumental in someone's death. Yet it is unlikely that someone would be thought mad or pathologically deranged who prayed for a person to live, and believed that such a prayer could cause that to be the case.

---

75. Quercus, 2013.

The difference, of course, is to do with the prayer itself. Prayer for someone to die a violent death is inconsistent with the purposes of a loving God, and so invoking him through prayer to perform an act so contrary to his nature might be described as insane, notwithstanding that he has the power to do it. Prayer predicated on God's power alone is theologically and morally unsustainable. Authentic prayer must always be offered on the assumption that God's power is qualified by God's love – something Gil Martin has to rediscover as his investigations come to a head . . .

Chapter five

Healing and wholeness: Prayer in practice

It was not by chance that our spectrum of possibilities relating to petitionary and intercessory prayer cited a prayer for healing by way of illustration. We pray for many things, but it is likely that prayers for healing and wholeness will feature most prominently in our individual and corporate intercessions. We may pray for the healing of people in their dis-ease of body, mind or spirit, or we may pray for the healing of relationships between individuals, communities and nations. We may pray for the restoration of wholeness on behalf of those experiencing the pain of loss and bereavement. In these and many other ways, the offering of impetratory prayer dovetails with the Church's ministry of healing, and so this ministry can be seen as a kind of case study whereby what we are doing when we pray finds practical expression through anointing and the laying-on of hands.

In my own case, it was through exercising the ministry of healing that I came to reflect more deeply on the meaning of and purport of prayer. It seemed to me that the same kinds of hopes and fears, expectation and desperation, fideism and superstition clustered around both the practice of prayer and the ministry of healing. Of course, the former has been taken for granted as a staple of Christian discipleship, while the latter has had a rather more chequered history. There are many reasons for this, but among them will surely be a suspicion that homing in on prayer for healing might be about putting prayer too precisely to the test, with a fear that it may in fact be found wanting. But it is for this reason that some focus on the ministry of healing, and the ways in which it is explained and interpreted, might help us to translate philosophical and theological categories into rather more pastoral considerations.

To set the scene, here is a short article written for our local church magazine to introduce a quarterly healing service:

What is a Healing Service?

Healing has been at the heart of the Christian gospel since those times 2000 years ago when Jesus healed people and empowered his followers to go and do likewise. Healing at the hands of Jesus was often miraculous and the Gospel story is studded with healing miracles. The Acts of the Apostles also contain many stories of miraculous healings. So what about today? People are still in need of healing, so how does healing fit into the ministry of our Church here in Haverfordwest?

Well, day by day in our acts of worship and in our private prayers we bring to God those we know to be in especial need of God's healing touch. Furthermore, those in need through sickness or sorrow are visited and cared for by clergy and members of our congregations. So the ministry of healing already has an honoured place in our life and witness as the people of God and the Body of Christ.

But now and again it is good to give this ministry special emphasis in a Healing Service, and I look forward to leading just such a service on Sunday

28 October at 5 p.m. in St Martin's Church. This is soon after St Luke's Day, and as we believe St Luke to have been a physician the timing is appropriate.

It will be a restful service taken at a steady pace so that each of us can concentrate on what God is wanting to say to us and do for us at this time. Those who wish to receive anointing with the laying-on of hands will be able to do so. This practice goes back to New Testament times and has proved a blessing to those who have received it. It may be that you yourself feel a particular need for healing, or you may come on behalf of someone else. Dis-ease of body, mind or spirit is familiar to all of us and so this ministry is God's gift to everyone with no questions asked or qualifications required.

Will miracles occur at such a service? They have been known. However, at the heart of it all is our need for wholeness which can be spiritual as well as physical. To experience healing is to experience the presence and peace of Christ in our own lives and in the lives of those we love. Faith, hope and love combine to strengthen and restore us so that we leave such a service encouraged by Jesus' words of gentle reassurance: go in peace, your faith has made you whole.

Here we notice some themes which have already featured in our consideration of petitionary and intercessory prayer:

- rooted in Scripture, the ministry of Jesus and Christian discipleship from the earliest days

- association with miracles

- implications for practical action
- relevance of relationships: ourselves, others, God
- about the whole person and not just what is physical

We also notice that what we have said about praying for all its worth applies equally to ministering healing for all its worth.

1. The healing is in the asking

If a prayer offered is a prayer received, then we can be confident that when we come for the laying-on of hands and anointing, this ministry is acceptable to God and is received graciously. That is certainly the conclusion we draw from the healing ministry of Jesus. Sometimes he simply found himself among people in search of healing, or they came to him specifically for that purpose. We also note the times when they were brought to him by friends or strangers. While he was thwarted by the scepticism and hostility of those he encountered in his home town, he otherwise welcomed those who came to him for healing even when he was seeking time to be alone. People's motives were not always spiritually pure or theologically precise, but that did not seem to matter. It is remarkable how Jesus credited people with faith who were certainly not seen as such by the religious authorities of the time – and we might wonder whether their credentials would pass muster in orthodox circles today! Few questions were asked, and no qualifications required, before a request for healing was received with grace and compassion. All who are minded to pray have access to the Father, and none who come to him for healing will be turned away.

These points need to be emphasised, because it is still likely that those who seek the Church's ministry of healing, especially if they are not church members or habitual worshippers, will be subject to a degree of circumspection. During the First World War, W. Studdert-Kennedy, or Woodbine Willie, spoke of a 'run on the bank of God'. He observed how many lost faith, some opted for occult ways, but most on all sides turned to God.

Is prayer 'a run on the bank of God' when it is prayer for healing or for peace in situations of hardship and distress? If it is, then the bank in question is certainly unique. For a start, the implication is that a bank is in danger of running out of funds, but God never runs out of love and mercy. During a banking crisis people compete to get there earlier, shout louder, knock harder and for longer to get their money. When it comes to God's healing love, there is always enough to go round. By no means least, a run on a bank is predicated on the money being our money and it is ours by right. However, life, wholeness and happiness are not ours by right. They are gifts to be longed for and prayed for, but not demanded. Healing is hoped for, and hope is not on ration. Hope is a currency common to our humanity and will not be despised by God who created us.

It is always tempting for the Church to stipulate conditions when it comes to who may or may not benefit from its healing ministry. The usual pre-condition is one of faith. Lack of faith disqualifies folk from accessing this ministry and/or provides an explanation when the specified cure does not occur. The reason for this is not difficult to understand. It arises from an anxiety to protect God's sovereignty. God must reserve the right to exercise his providential power on the basis of certain conditions, and having faith in his capacity to perform miraculous cures is his pre-requirement of choice.

But we have already asked ourselves whether God's sovereignty can or should be thought of in terms of his power when it is his will to have a loving relationship with us as made in his image, and gifted with free will, that really matters. Of course, God wants us to have faith in him as our Creator and Redeemer, but as Jesus demonstrated, what he is prepared to accept as the stuff of faith is much more generous in its nature than is usually allowed by those who attribute unanswered prayers or uncured ailments to a lack of faith. Hopes and fears, doubts and desperation, belief and unbelief, even simple-minded superstition, can get people within earshot of God in prayer and within touching distance of his healing hem.

So a request for healing is a request received, and a request received is, as we shall see, a request answered. And just as all are welcome at the throne of God's healing grace, so all that ails us is grist to the mill when it comes to the ministry of healing.

From the earliest years of the Christian era, oil has played a part in the Church's ministrations, including the ministry of healing. We continue to use oil in that ministry, together with its use in rites of initiation and ordination. These various uses reflect the way in which, for example, myrrh was administered in both the Old and New Testaments. Most well known is the use in anointing for burial: 'its bitter perfume breathes a life of gathering gloom; sorrowing,

sighing, bleeding, dying, sealed in the stone cold tomb'.[76]
It was also used as a painkiller, as in the case of Jesus on the
cross (Mark 15:23), and as a healing balm. In Psalm 45 it
becomes a perfume fit for a royal bride, signifying that she is
special and deserves to be singled out and celebrated. Then
there is the prostitute in Luke 7:36-50 who used myrrh to
anoint Jesus' feet. We know from Proverbs 7 that myrrh was
used by prostitutes to perfume the bed, so myrrh was essential
to her trade. Knowing this, her use of it to anoint Jesus takes
on a special poignancy. In scriptural terms, there seems to
be nothing which cannot be blessed by anointing with oil
and, likewise, virtually anything in our lives can be offered
to God for his healing touch. Dying and grieving, sickness
and pain, hopes and fears, sin and penitence, obligations and
responsibilities – all find us in equal need of God's grace, and
God's grace is equal to the needs of all.

Peter Baelz wondered whether:

there are some kinds of request that God is willing
to grant, and others that he is unwilling . . . Has he a
special list of his own approved charities? [77]

In relation to our petitions and intercessions we have argued
that whatever is of concern to us is of concern to God, and
he wants to hear about it and respond to it. So it is with
the ministry of healing. 'Come to me, all you who are weary
and burdened' (Matthew 11:28) remains the watchword, and
these are the terms on which this ministry is offered by the
Church and received by our Christlike God. The invitation to
come for healing is an open invitation, and to know ourselves

76. John Henry Hopkins (1820–91), 'We three Kings from Orient are'.
77. Baelz, *Does God Answer Prayer?*, p.5.

to be invited is to know ourselves to be received, and to be received into the presence of God is to find wholeness, whatever may befall:

> Just as I am, thou wilt receive,
> wilt welcome, pardon, cleanse, relieve:
> because thy promise I believe,
> O Lamb of God, I come. [78]

2. Healing is in what happens

To find wholeness, whatever may befall, is a bold ambition. It could be simply a matter of acquiescence to the fate that awaits us or has already befallen us. For many Christians, the best we can do is accept that how things are is how they must be, and compose ourselves accordingly. But we have not been prepared to see prayer in those terms, and we need not approach the ministry of healing on such a basis either.

Prayer makes a difference, and so does prayer for healing with the laying-on of hands and anointing. However, what we have said about the kinds of change effected by impetratory prayer must caution us against simplistic accounts of the kinds of change implicit in a healing ministry. It boils down to the difference between being cured and being healed, and to understanding that being healed is about being made whole.

When it comes to the difference between 'healing' and 'curing', we recognise that it is possible to receive either without the other. Nine lepers were cured but were not made whole – their wholeness depended on the degree of thankfulness which the tenth leper displayed and they did

---

78. Charlotte Elliott (1789–1871), 'Just as I am, without one plea'.

not (Luke 17:11-19). On the other hand, many are those who have not been physically cured but have yet achieved spiritual and emotional wholeness. This is something to which Paul testifies when he writes about his 'thorn in the flesh' which, along with the many other trials he had to undergo, enabled him to be strong even when he was weak (2 Corinthians 12:7-10). Saints through the centuries have had similar regard for the positive role of setback and suffering in their Christian formation, and most of us who have been in active ministry have found ourselves humbled and blessed by the evident wholeness of those beset by physical and emotional afflictions. While cures consequent upon the Church's ministry of healing are often claimed and celebrated, what is essentially being administered is the gift of wholeness so that whatever may befall the body, there is *shalom* for heart and soul.

The Hebrew word *shalom* captures the key ingredients of wholeness. 'The Lord be exalted, who delights in the well-being (*shalom*) of his servant,' says the psalmist (Psalm 35:27). Although the word is typically thought of as a synonym for 'peace', we are clearly being encouraged to see it as conveying much more than the absence of conflict. It is variously translated as good health, favour, prosperity, rest and, yes, wholeness. It can refer to the well-being of a city or community (Jeremiah 29:7), and it can have environmental implications (Isaiah 55:12). Yet at its heart this *port-manteau* word has the sense of being at ease with oneself, with those around us, with God our Creator and the creation fashioned in accordance with his will. When we minister healing, and experience this ministry for ourselves, we are sharing in

shalom, and when *shalom* is what happens, then healing as
wholeness will come to us like the rain, like 'spring rains that
water the earth' (Hosea 6:3).

3. Healing is in the doing

Our petitions and intercessions bring with them
responsibilities and obligations consistent with the
capabilities and opportunities we have to be part of the
answer to the prayers we offer. This means that the practice
of prayer is not a purely passive undertaking. And neither is
the experience of a healing ministry.

It is intriguing that when healing services happen on a
regular basis, a significant number of those who attend are
people who are likely to be active in sick visiting, pastoral
care and generally looking out for those in any kind of need.
Perhaps they use the healing ministry as a means whereby
they can themselves be strengthened and resourced with
that wholeness upon which their care and concern for others
depends. Perhaps it is the burdens they bear on behalf of others
that they are bringing with them to the place of anointing
and laying-on of hands. Either way, they are giving active and
practical expression to the symbiotic relationship between
our healing and diaconal ministries after the example of him
who came not to be served but to serve (Mark 10:45).

Of course, there will be those whose situation is such that
their capacity to offer an active ministry of care for others
is extremely limited. However, it will seldom be negated
altogether. W. H. Vanstone writes movingly about those
who minister to others when they themselves are severely

incapacitated, bedridden and sick unto death.[79] He highlights the passivity of Jesus after the arrest in Gethsemane, and especially when nailed to the cross. Even from there he reached out with words of reassurance to those around him. Significantly, the centurion, who can only have known Jesus at his most passive, is moved to acknowledge him as a son of God (Mark 15:39).

As wholeness is administered and received, it cannot but affect those who share this experience, and the relationship between them. The fact that touch plays an important part in the ministry of healing through the laying-on of hands may be something to do with this.

I recall a woman I met when I conducted her husband's funeral. She started coming to church regularly and although she never came forward for Communion, she received a blessing at the altar rail. She had not been confirmed, so when I approached her about being a candidate at an upcoming Confirmation service I was surprised by her determination not to put herself forward. Eventually I persuaded her to tell me why. She did not want to receive the bread and wine because then she would not receive a blessing, and she would miss that because, as she put it, 'That is the only time anyone touches me from one end of the week to the other.'

Touch is two way, and just as prayer affects those who pray as much as it affects those for whom prayer is offered, so the ministry of healing affects those who offer it as much as those who receive it. It is an interactive rather than an active–passive relationship, and there is healing in this interaction between

---

79. See W. H. Vanstone, *The Stature of Waiting* (Darton, Longman and Todd, 1982), pp.34ff.

two partners in the quest for wholeness – two beggars in search of bread.

4. Healing as self-sacrifice, solidarity and blessing

'Who touched my clothes?' asked Jesus as he sensed 'that power had gone out from him' when a woman with haemorrhages touched the hem of his garment (Mark 5:25-34). Ministering healing can take it out of you. It is self-sacrificial and entails an offering of oneself in the service of others. It can be quite exhausting – and if it's not, it should be! Because, as with prayer, it requires us to draw on our reserves of spiritual energy in ways that can be costly – or even very costly if we do not ensure that our spiritual wells are topped up on a regular basis.

One possible origin of the word 'ministry' is that it is the opposite of 'maxistry', from which the abbreviated form 'mastery' derives. Ministry is the opposite of mastery, and so forswears any pretensions to abnormal powers available for hire or sale. As we have seen, Jesus did not flaunt his healing powers. Unlike the itinerant healers prevalent at that time, he enjoined secrecy on those who witnessed his powers at work – it was not for the manifestation of those powers that he wanted to be sought after and followed.[80] His example reinforces the importance of those exercising a healing ministry simply making themselves available as channels of God's grace without any sense of personal charisma.

As a young curate, I was approached one day by a man who declared himself to possess special powers of healing; he offered his services to our church and community. An older and wiser priest, on overhearing this conversation, commented

---

80. See Rowan Williams, *Meeting God in Mark* (SPCK, 2014), p.35.

that the very fact that he was claiming to possess such powers was proof that he didn't. A bit harsh, perhaps, given that there is some evidence of certain individuals seeming to have particular gifts in relation to the ministry of healing. But his point was sound insofar as ministry is about making way for God to mediate wholeness through this ministry so that it effectively becomes his ministry and not ours. That degree of self-effacement does not always come easily to clergy and lay leaders, but it is necessary if God's will is to be done in us and through us – and even sometimes in spite of us.

So prayer and healing entail self-giving, as we give expression to our calling as cooperators with God in bringing to pass his providential purposes. And both entail solidarity. When we offer ourselves in a ministry of healing, we open ourselves to become channels of God's grace on behalf of others. Although we might look upon this as a natural outworking of our Christian discipleship, it has to be acknowledged that the historical relationship between Christianity and physical or mental infirmity has not always been that straightforward. There have been times when disfigurement or deformity has been considered an impediment to ordination and, of course, the persistence of beliefs in relation to demonic possession has resulted in mental illness being misunderstood, mistreated or even condemned as witchcraft. Those of us who witnessed an African bishop attempting to exorcise a gay man during the 1998 Lambeth Conference know only too well that such sentiments are still prevalent in some circles. Here was the ministry of laying-on of hands with prayer being perverted to become an expression of fear and hatred.

WHAT HAPPENS WHEN WE PRAY?

It is vital that we constantly reaffirm this ministry as an expression of solidarity with our sisters and brothers according to their needs – and especially towards those who are all too often marginalised by Church and society. This is the only way in which we can be true to the example of Jesus who notoriously reached out with his healing touch towards those whose social status, physical condition or mental state put them beyond the pale of acceptance and respectability. Not least among the ingredients of wholeness is to know ourselves to be fully human, made in the image of God, and accepted as such. The laying-on of hands with anointing and prayer is a tactile and tangible expression of this fundamental human right and needs to be celebrated accordingly.

Sometimes people fight shy of the Church's healing ministry because they are afraid of what others may think of them and what is 'wrong' with them. The temerity of the woman with haemorrhages is still a factor in how folk relate to this ministry. Let us be very clear: just as it is a pity not to feel able to bring everything to God in prayer, so it is a blight verging on blasphemy when someone feels that the healing ministry is not for the likes of them. That is not how we learned of Christ who summoned to himself ALL who travail and are heavy laden, and it is not how we learned of God's love which unites all humanity in its quest for life and life in all its fullness (John 10:10). Solidarity as a work of love is captured perfectly in Charles Edwin Markham's famous verse:

> He drew a circle to shut me out,
> heretic, rebel, a thing to flout.

But love and I had the wit to win,
we drew a circle that took him in.[81]

Widening the circle when it comes to how and for whom we pray, and to whom we minister healing, must be a priority for Christians committed to wholeness of body, mind and spirit. We need to know ourselves to be held and healed by the prayers of the Church, and others need to know that they are held and healed by our prayers, if we are to be truly in solidarity with one another as the Body of Christ.

That the ministry of healing is a blessing to those who share in it is beyond question. Such blessing is experienced by individuals, but it reaches further to touch communities and nations. A healing service will include opportunities for personal penitence and thanksgiving, and the laying-on of hands with anointing is an intensely personal experience. However, such services should also embrace wider concerns as we bring to God fractured relationships, divided communities and nations ravaged by war or civil unrest. Hunger and homelessness are constant threats to fullness of life, and victims of discrimination and injustice long for wholeness just as much as those who are physically ill and incapacitated. As our prayers for our local communities and the wider world are experienced as a blessing by those aware of them either consciously or subconsciously, so our ministry of healing embraces those caught up in troubles not of their making, but for whom the healing power of God's grace channelled through the Church's healing ministry can be a

81. Edwin Markham, 'Outwitted', in *The Shoes of Happiness, and Other Poems* (1913).

source of strength and reassurance. *Shalom* comes in many healthful guises, and *shalom* for one and for all is the blessing healing and wholeness confers as God wills.

5. Healing and waiting upon God

'As God wills' is a recurring phrase in any consideration of prayer and the ministry of healing. We have already set our face against any form of fatalism when it comes to praying, 'Thy will be done', because the obligations and responsibilities which go with the exercise of our free will cannot be so easily set aside. But that does not mean we should sit loose to waiting upon God in order to seek the will of God. Indeed, that is what Jesus did in Gethsemane, and our times of prayer, although usually less intense, are of the same order.

We may well approach petitionary and intercessory prayer with very clear ideas about what it is we want and need, and God has an ear for what we ask. But in the very process of prayer we place ourselves into a relationship with God which situates our supplications within a divine perspective where what happens is God's will underwritten by the virtues of faith, hope and love. Likewise, our hopes for healing are likely to be very clearly defined in our own minds, but in waiting upon God within the context of the Church's ministry of healing we set ourselves and our circumstances within an economy of grace and salvation which transcends anything we can fully comprehend.

In our times of waiting upon God there are three things which might especially concentrate our minds. First of all, we take time to reflect on those things for which we do well to give thanks to God, the Lord and giver of life. Popular songs exhort us to count our blessings, and the tone can sound overly sentimental or even a trifle mawkish. Yet there is virtue in giving thanks where thanks are due, and added value in facing the future with thankful hearts. When we sing Martin Rinkart's hymn 'Now thank we all our God', it is salutary to remind ourselves that he wrote it during his pastorate at Eilenburg in Saxony during the famine and pestilence of the Thirty Years' War. In the midst of such physical and emotional devastation he found much for which to be thankful, and that surely equipped him to be a minister of healing and wholeness in terrible times.

Secondly, in waiting upon God in the pregnant pauses which should always be part of a healing service, we have the opportunity to see health and safety in an entirely new light. The root meaning of 'safety' is the same as the root meaning of 'salvation'. To be safe is to be saved from harm, and it is significant that in the New Testament the same Greek word is used for both 'to save' and 'to heal'. So to be saved is to be truly safe, and to be truly safe is to experience healing and wholeness. What we mean by wholeness is always spiritual as well as physical, always psychological as well as somatic. For some, this feeling of being made whole comes with dramatic physical effects, and for everyone it comes with a sense of being safe – safe in the everlasting arms wherein is our salvation. By receiving the laying-on of hands we are putting ourselves and our loved ones into safe hands. Here is a whole new take on health and safety. Not the defensive, risk-averse and bureaucratically controlled world of restrictions and regulations, but a world in which to be in safe hands is to experience that quality of healing and wholeness which is beyond words and beyond price.

Thirdly, in waiting upon God we have the chance to think on who we are in relation to God and in the sight of God. In one of his New Year's Eve television messages, Archbishop Rowan Williams reflected on current environmental concerns and commented, 'God does not do waste!' This means that for everything and everyone there is a purpose and a destiny which is of God and is, therefore, always good. It is on this belief that healing is premised – and promised. It means that no one ever counts for nothing, so we come before God as we are that we may become as he would have us be. The gospel can be simply summarised as, 'God loves you as you are, and loves you too much to leave you that way.' And if God doesn't do waste, then nothing about us need go to waste. All our experiences, including those things we would wish had not happened, or had happened otherwise, are recycled and transformed. Some of the most effective ministers are those who have experienced much affliction in their lives but have been determined to recycle that experience as grist to the ministerial mill – because God does not do waste! Nothing God creates can or will ever be destroyed, but will be re-created and transformed. To this the resurrection of Jesus bears testimony, and therein lies our hope for healing and wholeness. In that hope we come to God:

> Just as we are, thou wilt receive,
> wilt welcome, pardon, cleanse, relieve:
> because thy promise we believe,
> O Lamb of God, we come.[82]

---

82. Elliott, 'Just as I am, without one plea'.

As we give thanks for God's gifts to us, take heart from God's care for us and make the most of God's will for us, we find ourselves in another and better place than when we first fell to our knees in prayer and sought solace in the ministry of healing and wholeness. When we wait upon God, what we want is transformed into God's will and, with Julian of Norwich, we can have the health-giving assurance that all shall be well, and all manner of things shall be well.[83]

6. Healing and our relationship with God

Petitionary and intercessory prayer is premised on the belief that God wills to exercise his providential options in the light of requests made in all good faith, and to which he responds. Furthermore, when we make those requests we do so not with an eye so much on God's power as on his love. This is the essence of the relationship God wants with us, and it underpins every aspect of prayer as we have come to understand it – Adoration, Confession, Thanksgiving and Supplication. By extension, it is such a relationship which informs the ministry of healing. Remember the Chicago pastor when you are invited to receive the laying-on of hands with anointing: 'The worst thing that can happen to you is that you will have an experience of being profoundly loved.' The fact of the matter is that we do not know ourselves to be loved because we have experienced healing; we experience healing because we know ourselves to be loved.

A key word in telling the tale of God's power in love with the world is 'compassion'. It is a relational word carrying no sense of unilateral action. Rather, it expresses responsiveness

83. Julian of Norwich, *Revelations of Divine Love* (Penguin, 1966), p.109.

on the part of one party to the needs of another where those needs have been made known by them or by others on their behalf. Repeatedly in the Gospels Jesus shows such compassion, and it is always personal and appropriate, never automatic or formulaic. It is God's kindly, costly compassion which gives expression to his character as power in love with the world.

We can summarise much of what we have been trying to say about the ministry of healing by dwelling for a while on this quality of compassion and the promise it holds for us and for others as we long for wholeness in a sadly dis-eased and fragmented world.

The economy of compassion involves a sequence of three steps – theologians call them cognitive, affective and volitional or, more simply,

- We notice another's need.
- We feel another's need.
- We act on another's need.

So let us take in turn those three steps in the economy of Christian compassion, and relate them to the Church's ministry of healing.

a. Compassion is noticing another's need

At Nazareth, Jesus noticed the needs of the world around him – and in his Synagogue sermon he gave notice that needs of the poor, the imprisoned, the blind and the broken in body, mind or spirit would be the mainstay of his mission (Luke 4:14-21). And so the Church through her ministry of healing notices the corporate and individual needs of society, and serves notice that those needs will not be ignored. This is the first step in the Christian economy of compassion.

b. Compassion feels another's need

Compassion entails suffering with and for another person or other people. We sacrifice something of ourselves for the sake of the other – the self-centred security blanket with which we surround ourselves is set aside in response to the pain and sorrow of someone other than ourselves. In Gethsemane Jesus not only noticed such need, but he also *felt* the full force of it as he agonised over the cost of compassion. It was Roman practice to anoint athletes before they were put to the test in trials of strength and endurance. This time of tension before the event the Greeks called *agonia* – the agony Jesus underwent in the Garden.

So we anoint the newly baptised with oil to strengthen their reserves of faith and love for the way ahead. We anoint the newly confirmed with oil to strengthen their resolve to continue in the way they have chosen as disciples of Christ. And we anoint the sick with oil that they may be strengthened by the companionship and compassion of Christ and his Church. Touch plays a key part in our healing ministry: through anointing and the laying-on of hands we not only notice the other's need but we also feel it, and we pray that God's peace and power to heal is felt in return. This feeling for and with another human being in their need for wholeness is the second step in the Christian economy of compassion.

c. Compassion acts on another's need

On the cross of Calvary we see the culmination of all Christ's acts of compassion towards the leper, the deaf man, the bereaved parent, the epileptic boy and the man born blind. Jesus not only noticed and felt the needs of the world; he also gave himself for them in that conclusive manifestation of love's endeavour and love's expense. Disablement and death were ultimately challenged and dethroned in a titanic three-day trial of strength from Good Friday to Easter Day. So the Church through her ministry of healing not only notices the needs of people for wholeness, and feels that need, but works tirelessly to address that need through countless individual acts of pastoral care as well as through prayerful and prophetic challenges to the unjust structures of society. Thus willing and working for the wholeness of individuals, communities, nation and creation, the Church takes the third step in the Christian economy of compassion.

So what *does* happen when we pray?

What happens when we pray? A relationship is fostered between God as creator and sustainer of all that is, and his human creatures called into being precisely so as to forge this reciprocal and mutually enriching relationship.

It is a relationship which strikes a balance between God's sovereignty and our freedom, whereby both we and God embrace self-limitation in order to promote life in all its fullness. It is a relationship which sets making our requests known to God as the key to understanding how God continues to act providentially in the world – and how we both affect and are affected by God's providence. It is a relationship which embraces all of our humanity in such a way that there is nothing we cannot bring to God in prayer, and nothing we bring to God in prayer ever counts for nothing.

A prayer offered is a prayer received, and a prayer received is a prayer answered. It is a relationship which enables time to interact with eternity so that we, like Abraham Lincoln, are driven to our knees by the overwhelming conviction that there is, quite literally, nowhere else to go.

Also by John Saxbee

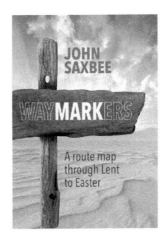

WayMARKers
A route map through Lent to Easter
1501418

www.kevinmayhew.com